More Snoopy® Collectibles

An Unauthorized Guide   Revised & Expanded 2nd Edition

Jan Lindenberger   with Cher Porges

Schiffer Publishing Ltd®

4880 Lower Valley Road, Atglen, PA 19310 USA

ACKNOWLEDGMENTS

I wish to give a very special thank you to Cher Porges and her family. Without Cher the Snoopy books would not have been possible. We worked many weeks and long hours to give this project the value it deserves. Her patience in arranging and rearranging her vast collection was greatly appreciated. In the process she says that she found things she had forgotten were there. The information for this price guide came from her years of knowledge and research.

Between diet sodas and mustard pretzels and the privilege of me sleeping near "The Snoopy room", *The Unauthorized Guide to Snoopy Collectibles* and this book, *More Snoopy Collectibles: An Unauthorized Guide,* were born.

Together we worked hard to provide much needed, all color information and price guides to Snoopy collectibles. So again I thank Cher. It was wonderful working with you and I have gained you and your family as my valued friends. That's the best part of this job.

Thanks also to Laurel Sherry from New Holstein, Wisconsin. Laurel is the show promotor for the Mid West Snoopy Swap Meet. She allowed me to photograph on show and encouraged me to do this book. Thanks too, to all the dealers at the show that let me photograph their Snoopy's. For information about the Snoopy swap meet contact Laurel by phone at 902-898-5578.

Nancy Wilke, Chesterfield, Missouri, gave Cher and I a day's worth of hard work and spent many hours on the phone with Cher giving us valuable information. Thanks, Nancy. Thanks also to: Warren Chamberlin, Mishawauka, Indiana; Kevin Knauer, Colorado Springs, Colorado; and Joel Martone, Colorado Springs, Colorado.

Revised price guide: 2000
Copyright © 1997 & 2000 Jan Lindenberger
Library of Congress Catalog Card Number: 99-68312

Designed Bonnie M. Hensley

ISBN: 0-7643-0881-5
Printed in China
1 2 3 4

Published by Schiffer Publishing Ltd.
4880 Lower Valley Road
Atglen, PA 19310
Phone: (610) 593-1777; Fax: (610) 593-2002
E-mail: Schifferbk@aol.com
Please visit our web site catalog at **www.schifferbooks.com**

In Europe, Schiffer books are distributed by Bushwood Books
6 Marksbury Avenue Kew Gardens
Surrey TW9 4JF England
Phone: 44 (0)208-392-8585; Fax: 44 (0)208-392-9876
E-mail: Bushwd@aol.com

This book may be purchased from the publisher.
Include $3.95 for shipping. Please try your bookstore first.
We are interested in hearing from authors with book ideas on related subjects.
You may write for a free printed catalog.

CONTENTS

INTRODUCTION

Welcome to *More Snoopy Collectibles*. Even when I was working on *The Unauthorized Guide to Snoopy Collectibles* I was sure that I would never cover every thing. And, of course, this isn't the entire number or variety of Snoopy collectibles that were ever produced or that are available today. Everyday something new enters the market, so the best I can do is to provide the collector up-to-date and general information and a current price guide for this lovable beagle.

Snoopy is the creation of Charles Monroe Schulz. Always a lover of cartoons, Schulz was even nicknamed Sparky, after the horse in the Barney Google comics. Schulz pursued cartooning through a "mail order" art school, and then began teaching for the same school. In 1950 he traveled to New York and United Features Syndicate to offer them his "L'il Folks" comic strip. They liked the concept and changed the name to "Peanuts." They also tried to limit the role of the dog, Snoopy. Schulz stood by his guns and Snoopy became the central character of the Peanuts gang.

The love of Snoopy is universal. Around the world people love the characters, and as you will see in this book, the comic strip and the products it has inspired are translated into many languages.

The character of Snoopy has changed immensely over the years. You can tell this by his five different two-dimensional copyright dates. When Snoopy first appeared in 1950 he always walked on four feet or sat on his haunches. This was his earliest copyright date. He earned another copyright in 1956 when he was shown dancing on two feet with his head high. He was walking on two feet all the time by 1958, thus earning his third copyright date. His fourth copyright date came in 1965, with his ears tucked under his aviators hat and goggles covering his eyes, he began his battles as the Flying Ace, fighting his nemesis the Red Baron. His final copyright date came in 1971, when Joe Cool appeared on the scene. Yet through all these changes he kept his lovable personality and his enduring charm.

Cher Porges resides in Fenton, Missouri, with her husband Tony and two children, Drew and Concetta. Also sharing her home are two beagles named Joe Cool and Woodstock 2. She is a more than avid collector of Snoopy. Cher has been collecting this wonderful beagle most of her life. Her home is surrounded with "Snoopy" memorabilia, Woodstock and The Peanuts gang, amounting to well over 5000 items.

HINTS FOR COLLECTORS

By far the best place to buy Snoopy Collectibles is the Mid West Snoopy Swap Meet. This show and sale is organized by Laurel Sherry. One may contact Laurel at 1723 Monroe St. New Holstein, Wisconsin. 53061 for information on the next meet. Or phone at 920-898-5578, Fax 920-898-1325, E-mail: cowtown@fdldotnet.com, www.fdldotnet.com/~cowtown.

Several hundred people who love Snoopy get together to buy, sell, trade and talk Snoopy. You will find Snoopy and the Peanuts Gang in abundance. The prices are more than fair and the spirit among the sellers is very cheerful. To the collector, it's better than Christmas. You can tell they all love that beagle!

Searching for Snoopy is fun and challenging. While waiting for the Snoopy Swap Meet, a good way to start a collection is to scour garage sales and flea markets. The prices are usually negotiable but the merchandise isn't always mint. The more flaws the less you should have to pay.

Antique Malls can also be fruitful. Prices vary extremely but, depending on condition and how knowledgeable the seller is, mer-chandise can be reasonably had. If the item catches your eye and you must have it, it's quite convenient to purchase it at the mall or antique shop. Remember the old slogan, "You snooze, you lose?" Purchase it when you see it or it may not be there when you go back.

If you have a bit more cash, toy shows are wonderful. Prices can be negotiated slightly and merchandise is generally in good condition. There are also several toy magazines which have adver-tisements from all over the country. This is a good way to track down hard-to-find treasures.

For new items a good source, especially around the holiday season when special things come on the market, is Knotts Berry Farms, Camp Snoopy.

Whatever path you choose to take in your search for Snoopy, remember the real search is for fun!

I hope you enjoy this Snoopy collectibles guide. Prices may vary according to area, availability, and condition. Please take this book with you on your "Snoopy search" and happy hunting!

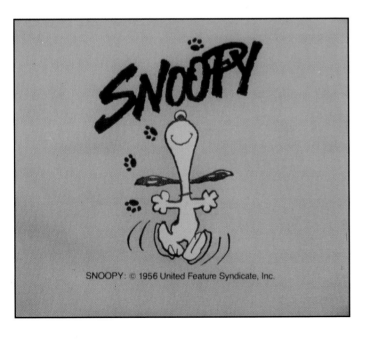

SNOOPY: © 1956 United Feature Syndicate, Inc.

BIBLIOGRAPHY

Johnson, Rheta Grinslay. *Good Grief: The Story of Charles Schulz.* New York: Pharos Books, 1989. Pharos Book. New York.

Fanning, Jim. *Boomer Magazine*, April, 1995. Dubuque, Iowa: Antique Trader Publicatons. Dubuque, Iowa.

Holt, Charles M. *You Don't Look 35 Charlie Brown.* New York: Holt, Rinehart, Winston, 1985.

LIVING WITH SNOOPY

TROPHIES

Aviva trophies total well over 100. They were produced in large quantities throughout the 1970s and into the 1980s. While they portrayed the entire Peanuts gang, Snoopy and Woodstock were the most represented. Snoopy being the most common, unless unusual, $8-10. Variations include a larger scenic trophy, early 1970s, $15-20. Sparkies were mounted on teakwood base without message. 1971/1972, $25-35.

"Happiness Is A Good Friend" trophy. Aviva. $8-12

"America You're Beautiful" trophy. Aviva. $12-18

"Happy Monday!" trophy. Aviva. $8-12

"World's Biggest Clown" trophy. Aviva. $8-12

"World's Best Driver" trophy. Aviva. $8-12

"World's Greatest Bowler" trophy from Aviva. 1970s-80s. $8-12

"World's Greatest Tennis Player" trophy. Aviva. $8-12

"World's Greatest Golfer" trophy from Aviva. 1970s-80s. $8-12.

"Happiness Is Me And You" trophy. Aviva. $8-12

"You're the Joe Coolest" trophy. Aviva. $8-12

"Joe Rembrandt" trophy. Aviva. $8-12

"Think Snow" trophy. Aviva. $8-12

JOE REMBRANDT

"You're A Real Winner" trophy. Aviva. $8-12

Santa Snoopy trophy in box. Aviva. 1980s. $18-25

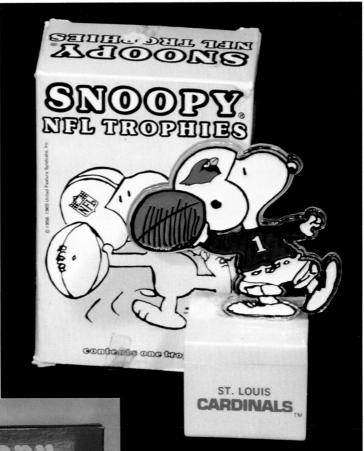

Plastic Snoopy NFL trophy. Mid-1980s. 28 different team trophies were produced. Made by Quantasia. $15-20

Scenic trophy, plastic Snoopy, the skier. Aviva. $18-25

Scenic trophy, plastic cupid Snoopy with Woodstock. Aviva. $18-25

Wall plaque, Snoopy dancing with Woodstock from Hallmark. 3" x 4.5". 1970s. $5-7

"The Grade A Teacher Award." Hallmark. 1980s. $5-7

Hallmark wall plaque, Snoopy with friend Woodstock. 6" x 6". 1970s. $8-12

Round wall plaque. "Merry Christmas, Teacher." 1982. Hallmark. 3" x 4.5". $6-8

Wall plaque. "Happy Today." Hallmark. 3" x 4.5". 1970s. $5-7

Hallmark wall plaque, Snoopy hugging Woodstock. 7" x 7". 1980s. $8-12

Hallmark wall plaque, Snoopy bringing a flower to Woodstock. 5" x 7". 1980s. $8-12

Hallmark wall plaque, Snoopy with trophy and Woodstock. 3" x 4.5". 1990s. $5-7

Mirror, Snoopy and Woodstock, wood frame. Determined. England. 8" x 10". 1970s. $35-45

Mirror, "I think I'm alergic to morning!" Wood frame. Determined. England. 8" x 10". 1970s. $35-45

Snoopy enamel on metal, picture frames from Butterfly. 1979. $20-30 each.

Mirror, "Who's the Coolest Of Them All?" Plastic frame by Determined. 8" x 10". 1980s. $15-25

Picture holder from Butterfly. Opens like a compact. Late 1970s. $20-30

Metal enamel heart-shaped Snoopy frame by Butterfly. 1979. $20-30

Snoopy metal picture frames. 1980s. $15-25 each.

Production cel from Saturday morning cartoon series, the "Charlie Brown and Snoopy Show." 1980s. Framed, triple matted. $500-750

Joe Ranger picture frame with package. 1980s. $15-20

"Let The Good Times Roll" Plastic picture frame. 1980s. $10-15

Stained glass Snoopy ornament from Oden. 1980. 5.5", $35-45. 3.5", $30-40. Not shown: Snoopy howling at a crescent moon, $45-55; Snoopy dancing, $25-35; Snoopy sitting, 5.5": $25-35, 4.75": $20-30; Joe Cool, 4.5", $25-35; Snoopy with yellow parachute, 8.5", $40-50; Snoopy laying on red heart, $35-45; Snoopy sitting with Woodstock, $35-45; Flying Ace, $35-45; Snoopy on doghouse with Woodstock on his tummy, 6.75", $40-50; Snoopy sits next to supper dish with Woodstock in dish, $35-45

Leaded glass Snoopy window, Hand made by Clayton Anderson, Andy Crafts. 1980s. $600-750

Joe Cool painted window hanging stained glass illusion. 5" x 7". Aviva. 1981. $25-35. Not shown: Flying Ace, Joe Gourmet, Snoopy and Woodstock with balloons. $25-35 each

Needlepoint Snoopy on skis. Malina. Late 1970s. $15-20 each

Snoopy-Joe Cool sunshiner from Aviva. Late 1970s. $15-20

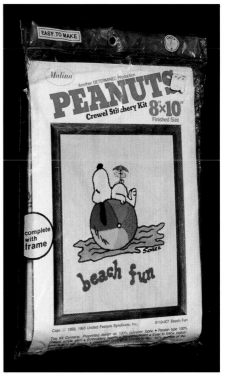

Embroidered Snoopy wall set. Color stitch kits for kids, completed. JCA, late 1980s-1990s. $10-15 each

Malina Stitchery Kit. Mint package. Early 1980s. $25-50. Completed mint. $30-75. Came in a large variety of sizes and techniques, crewel, needlepoint, stitchery.

Embroidered Snoopy wall set. Color stitch kits for kids, completed. JCA, late 1980s-1990s. $10-15 each.

Color stitch kit for kids, late1980s. JCA, Inc. $10-15 each.

Snoopy on stick horse, cork bulletin board. Manton Cork Corp. 1980s. $15-25

Cork bulletin board. Manton Cork Corp. 1980s. $15-25

Snoopy reading paper, cork bulletin board. Manton Cork Corp. 1980s. $15-25

Felt Snoopy banner. 1970s. Determined Products. $15-25

Peanuts Fall Decorations from Hallmark. Late 1980s early 1990s. $4-7

Peanuts Football Press-out Decorations. Hallmark. 1970s. $15-20

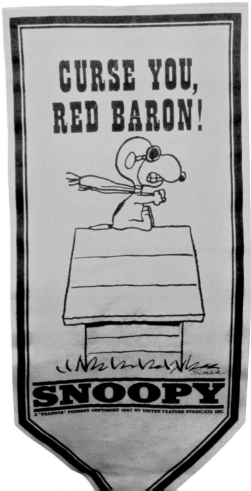

Felt Flying Ace banner. 1970s. Determined Products. $15-25

Felt banners. Determined Products. 1970s. $15-25 each.

Felt Snoopy and Woodstock banner. 1970s. Determined Products. $15-25

Felt Snoopy banner. 1970s. Determined Products. $15-25

Felt banner. "Snoopy for President." Determined. 1970s. $15-20

Linen towel. "Snoopy for Prime Minister." 20" x 30". 1980s. Made in United Kingdom. $25-35

Felt calendar. 1983. Bucilla kit, jeweled. $25-35

Mylar banners. Mid-1990s. 34.75"
x 5". $3-4 each.

Nylon embroidered Snoopy on doghouse
flag. 1995. $20-25

Plastic door knockers. Butterfly. Late 1970s.
$7-14 each.

Nylon screen printed Joe Cool flag. 1996. $10-15

FLOOR STUFF

Peanuts Latch Hook Kit. Came with rug inside.
Malina, 1970s. $35-45

Latch hook Christmas rug of Snoopy and
Woodstock from Malina, made from a kit.
1970s. $35-45

Malina Latch Hook Kit. Weight lifter Snoopy. 1970s.
18" x 24". $35-45

Latch hook Snoopy in suit, rug from Malina Co. Made from kit. Early
1980s. $35-45

Cotton weave throw rug. Do not disturb Snoopy. $20-30

Latch hook Snoopy jogging rug from Malina Co. Made from a kit. Early 1980s. $35-45

In the 1990s, Frank T. Greco Inc. produced a large, reasonably priced selection of cotton throw rugs that could be utiized for floor or wall decoration. These high quality handmade and individually screen printed rugs came in various sizes with different scenes depicted. 22" x 40". 20" x 34".

Cotton weave throw rug. Flying Ace. $20-30

Cotton weave throw rug. Snoopy in sports car. $20-30

Cotton weave throw rug. Snoopy with train. $20-30

Rubber "Happy Holidays" door mat. 1980-90s. $30-40

Rubber personalized door mat. 1980s. $30-40

Welcome mat, indoor or outdoor. Bacova Guild Ltd. Olefin carpets. 1990s. $15-20

Welcome mat, Snoopy and Woodstock. Bacova Guild Ltd. Olefin carpets. 1990s. $15-20

Acrylic plush Snoopy cowboy, rug. 1990s. $20-30

BOOK STUFF

Ceramic pair of Snoopy bookends. $40-50

Ceramic Snoopy sitting bookends. Butterfly. $30-50

Rubber bookends. Woodstock and Snoopy on heart shaped base. Butterfly, 1981. $25-35

Ceramic train bookends. Willitts. 1990. $40-60

TEA TIME

Ceramic teapot. Late 1990s. Japan. $40-75

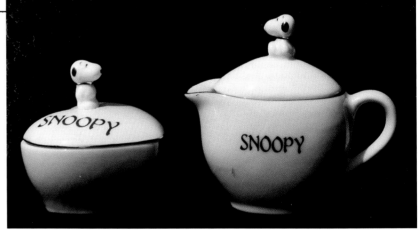

Porcelain sugar/creamer with blue and 14K trim. Late 1990s. Japan. Sankyo Original. $50-75 set.

OUTDOOR STUFF

Bird feeder featuring Snoopy on dog house with Woodstock on the perch. Con Agra Inc. Early 1980s. $30-40 with box.

Snoopy giant thermometer by Sybron/ Taylor. 11" x 12" 1979. $50-75 with box.

BABY STUFF

Kolcraft infant walker with detachable toy bar. In the late 1980s/ early 90s Kolcraft made a darling line of baby/infant products. Pictured here and in another section are the walker and infant car seat carrier. Also seen are the high chair, older infant/ toddler car seat, and crib mattress. Walker. Mint in box. $40-75

Snoopy vinyl and chrome high chair. 1970s. (Also made was a playpen, vinyl bumper pad and an old fashioned pumpkin seat in this pattern). Mint chair. $60-100

LIFE IS FOR THE DOGS!

"Fetching Cologne for Precious Pets." Snoopy Private Collection. "A Rugged, Spicy Scent." $12-18

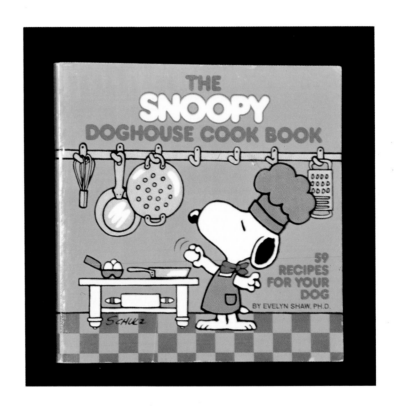

The Snoopy Doghouse Cookbook. Evelyn Shaw, PH.D. 1980s. $12-18

Plastic Snoopy dishes. Determined. Early 1970s. 5". $10-20 each.

Plastic Snoopy dog dish by Determined. Came in a varity of colors and 5" and 7" sizes. 1970s. $10-20

Plastic Snoopy dog dish by Determined. Came in a variety of colors and 5" and 7" sizes. 1970s. $10-20

Ceramic dog dish. A bone sits inside. 1994. Benjamin and Medwin. $25-35

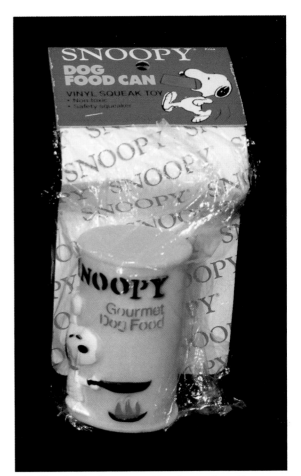

Rubber dog food can, squeaking dog toy from Conagra Pet Products. 1980s-90s. $4-6

Snoopy surrounded by a Christmas wreath, squeaking vinyl dog toy. Con Agra, 1980s-1990s. $4-6

Snoopy plastic feeding dog mat. 1990s. $6-8

Joe Cool squeaking vinyl dog toy. Con Agra, 1980s-90s.. $4-6

Flying Ace squeaking dog toy from Conagra Pet Products. 1980s-1990s. $4-6

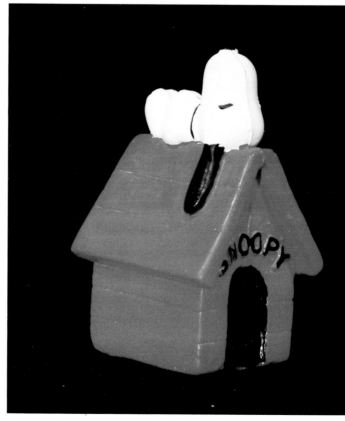

Jogging Snoopy squeeking vinyl dog or baby toy. Danara. 1980s. $5-8

Snoopy on house squeaking dog toy from Conagra Pet Products. 1980s-90s. $4-6

Rubber Snoopy squeaking dog toy from Conagra Pet Products. 1980s-90s. $4-6

Rubber shoe squeaking dog toy from Conagra Pet Products. 1980s-90s. $4-6

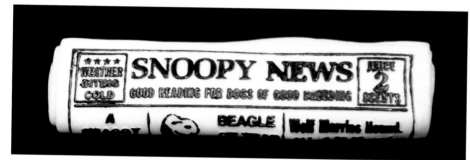

Rubber newspaper squeaking dog toy from Conagra Pet Products. 1980s-90s. $4-6

Dog toy. China. It even squeaks! Late 1990s. $6-8

SNOOPY'S SCHOOLTIME

PAPER STUFF

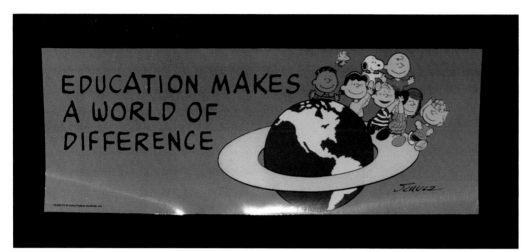

Advertising poster for education. 1990s.
$5-7

Gymnast Snoopy, ring binder. Butterfly. 1970s. $10-15

Notebook ring binder with Snoopy and Woodstock.
Butterfly. Early 1980s. $10-15

Snoopy climbing rock notebook. Butterfly. 1980s. $10-15

Paper note pads. 1980s-90s. $2-3 each

Snoopy score pad. Hallmark. Complete playing card ensemble came with box, two decks of matching cards, score pad, and a mechanical pencil. Mid-1970s. $35-45

Snoopy and Woodstock ring binder. Butterfly. 1970s. $10-15

Scratch pads. Hallmark. Snoopy,1980s, $8-11. Sally, 1990s, $5-6

Snoopy cover booklet of note cards. Hallmark. 1970s. Complete booklet, $15-25

Snoopy friend to friend note cards. One of many in booklet.

Snoopy note cards. One of a booklet.

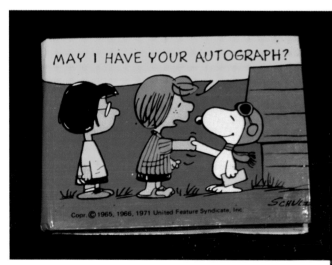

Peanuts Gang autograph book. Butterfly. 1970s. $7-12

In the 1970s Butterfly produced a large variety of 'minis'. Wha was so wonderful about them? Just darling miniature versions c ordinary things and they were so reasonably priced. Original price were only as high as a few dollars.

Peanuts Gang mini-memo pads. Butterfly. 1970s. $5-7 each

Woodstock pocket notebook. Butterfly.
1970s. $5-7

UltimateMemo, magnetic and wipe off board from Manton. 1980s.
5-20

Vinyl Peanuts Roll Call, a mini clip notebook from Butterfly.
1970s. $5-7

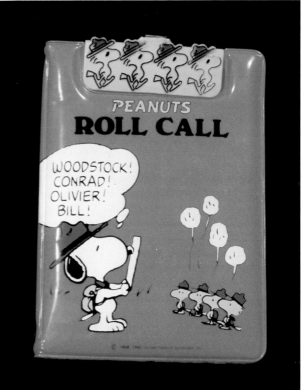

oopys mini note pad and pad and pencil set. Butterfly. 1970s.
-7 each

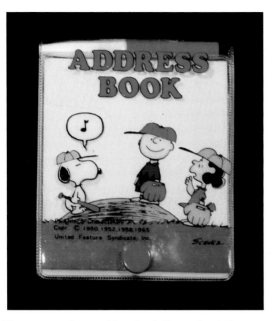

Plastic covered mini address book. Butterfly. 1970s. $4-6

Mini notes. Butterfly. 1970s. $4-6

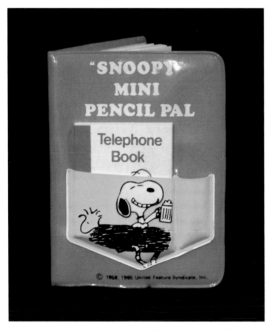

Plastic "Snoopy Mini Pencil Pal Telephone Book." Butterfly mini. 1970s. $5-7

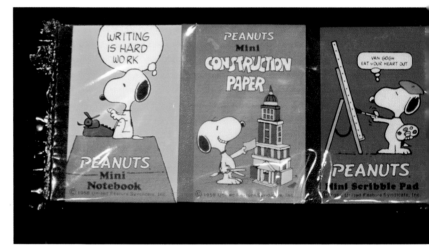

Mini Peanuts paper set. Butterfly. 1970s. $6-8

"Plastic Wipe Off" note board. Butterfly. 1970s. $5-7

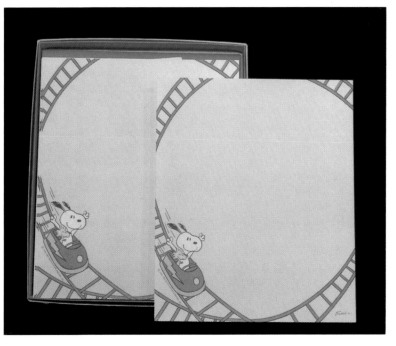

Boxed mini-stationary with envelopes. Hallmark. 1990s. $20-25 complete set.

"Snoopy Pocket Dividers." Plymouth Inc. manufactured for Butterfly. 1980s. $6-8

Snoopy boxed stationary. Hallmark. 1980s. Mint/boxed, complete with envelopes. $20-25 set

"Peanuts Letter Set." Butterfy mini. 1970s. $5-7

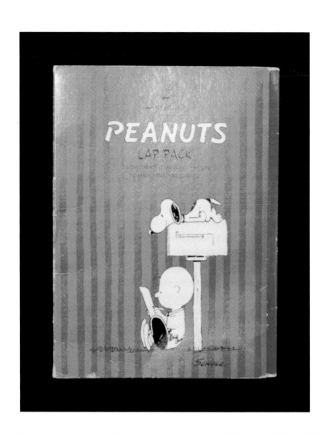

"Peanuts Lap Pack." Note paper, envelopes. Hallmark, 1970s. $20-25 complete

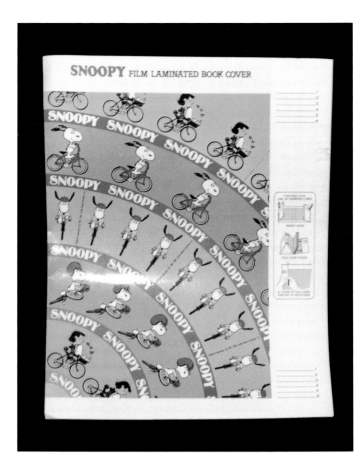

Laminated book cover. Plymouth Inc. Manufactured for Butterfly. 1980s. $4-6

WRITING STUFF

Snoopy boxes of crayons. Butterfly. Early 1980s. $5-7 each in mint condition.

Plastic Snoopy pencil holders filled with colored pencils or regular pencils. Empire Berol, 1990s. $5-8 each.

Set of 12 color pencils. Empire Berol Co. 1980s. $5-7

Gold Snoopy gold-filled pen in tin case. Stylus. 1995. $25-30

Snoopy pen and pencil sets. Empire/Empire Berol. 1980s-90s. $3-6 set each.

"Peanuts Pens." 6 pack of Snoopy pens. $15-25. 4 pack of party pens, Peanuts gang. Sunkisses Hawaii Ltd. $10-15

Plastic pencil cases. Hallmark, early 1980s. $8-12 each.

Snoopy "Mini Pencil Set." Butterfly. 1970s. $5-7

Plastic "Mini Pencil Case." Butterfly. 1970s. $4-6

Snoopy 1980 calendar. $20-25

Tin Snoopy heart-shaped box. Filled with rubber stamp and ink etc. Japan. Butterfly. 1980s. $15-20

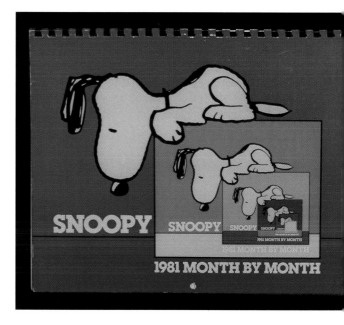

"Snoopy 1981 Monthly Calendar." 1980. $20-25

Opposite page
Top left: "Snoopy 1992 Calendar." $10-15

Center left: Snoopy and Woodstock sticker calendar. Ambassador. 1995. $10-15

Bottom left: Hallmark Peanuts desk calendar. 1995. $15-20

Plastic school supplies. Pen holder and book mark. Butterfly. 1970s. $5-7 each

Plastic paper clip in the shape of a cloths pin. Butterfly. 1970s. $3-5

Plastic Snoopy stapler. Butterfly. 1970s. $7-9

Plastic paper clips featuring the Peanuts Gang. Mini clamps sold in packages as a set. Paper clips sold as a set also. 1970s. $6-8 set

Snoopy office supplies. Tape dispenser or glue. Butterfly. 1970s. $5-7 each

Rubber stamper kits. The Rubber Stamp Factory. 1990s. $7-20 each.

Plastic Peanuts Gang ruler. Butterfly. 1980s. $4-6

Plastic ruler. Snoopy and friends. 1980s. $3-5

Plastic pencils/pen holders. 1990s. $6-10 each.

Stick on looseleaf reinforcements. Butterfly.1980s. $4-6

Plastic pencil sharpener.
Maker unknown. 1980s.
$20-30

Plastic paper clips from Japan. 1990s. $5-7

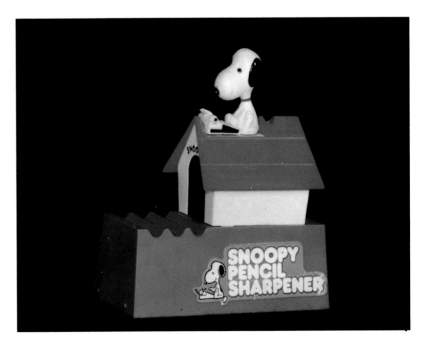

Snoopy on doghouse pencil sharpener. Kenner. Battery operated. 1974.
$45-60 in box

Refrigerator magnets. Wecolite. 1980s-90s. $3-5 per card

Magnets. Magnetic Collectibles Ltd. 1990s. $3-5 each. Also available in shrink wrapped package.

Variety of cities refrigerator magnets. Mid-1990s. Magnetic Collectibles Ltd. $3-5 each

Variety of cities refrigerator magnets. Mid-1990s. Magnetic Collectibles Ltd. $3-5 each

Variety of Christmas refrigerator magnets. Mid-1990s. Magnetic Collectibles Ltd. $3-5 each

Variety of sports refrigerator magnets. Mid-1990s. Magnetic Collectibles Ltd. $3-5 each

Plastic "Snoopy Play Smock." Empire Pencil. 1980s.
$7-10 each.

Magnetic bulletin board containing Snoopy magnets of various
materials. Ceramic, vinyl, rubber and plastic. 1980-1990s. $3-8 each.

Japanese vinyl sticker. 4.5" x 2.5". 1990s. $5-7

Wooden rubber stamps. Rubber Stampede
depending on size. 1980s. $6-15 each.

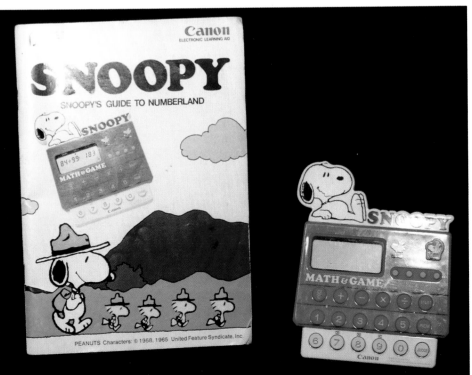

Canon calculator and instructions.
1980s. $25-35

Plastic Snoopy lunch box, King Seeley Thermos. 1980s. $20-25

Cardboard lunch box, Snoopy's doghouse. Dolly Madison promotion. 1970s. $10-12

Metal Peanuts lunch box, King Seeley Thermos. 1980s. $25-35

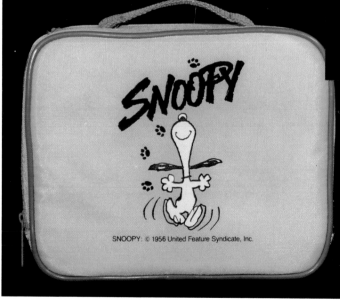

Nylon Snoopy lunch tote with King Seeley Thermos. Mid-1990s. $15-20

Plastic Snoopy lunch box, King Seeley Thermos. 1980s. $20-25

Metal Snoopy lunch box, King Seeley
Thermos. Late 1960s. $35-50

Metal lunch box. Snoopy and
Woodstock on swing. Japan. 1990s.
$20-30

Nylon insulated tote. 1980s. $15-20

Plastic flashing key chains. Hallmark. Early 1970s. $15-20 each.

Brass "Ski," Snoopy key chain. Quantasia. 1980s. $7-10

Plastic "Snoopy Fan Club," key chain. Quantasia. 1980s. $6-8

Plastic Flying Ace key chain. Made exclusively for Knotts Berry Farms by Brabo Group. 1990s. $3-5

Plastic square Snoopy and Woodstock key chain. 1980s. Aviva. $5-7

Plastic Snoopy and Woodstock key chain. Monogram Products. 1990s. $4-6

Joe Cool, rubber key chain. Accessory Network. Mid-1990s. $4-6

Plastic Snoopy, initial key chain. 1990s. Monogram Products. $4-6

Plastic airplane key chain. Japan. 1990s. $5-7

Plastic skating Snoopy key chain. Monogram Products. 1990s. $4-6

Plastic snowman and Snoopy key chain. Quantasia. 1980s. $6-8

Snoopy key chain. Applause. 1990s. $4-6

SNOOPY'S LIBRARY

READ TO ME!

Peanuts, 1952 and *Snoopy*, 1958 by Charles Schulz. Paperback. Rinehart & Co. Inc. $3-20 each depending on condition and edition.

Snoopy greeting card. 1980s. $3-4

The Gospel According to Peanuts by Robert L. Shorts. John Knox Press. 1965. Paperback $8-12. Hardback $20-25

3 Snoopy books by Charles Schulz from Hallmark. Each book is part of a different set. *Peanut Philsophy*, 1972. Other books in this set but not shown are *Linus on Life*, *The Wisdom of Charlie Brown*, and *The World According to Lucy*. They came in a cardboard case. $30-40 set or $10-15 each. *More Peanuts Philosophy* was also issued in 1972. *A Friend Is...*,1972. $10-15. Other books in this set were *All About Birthdays*, 1971, $10-15 and *All About Friendship*, 1968, $10-15. *The Wit and Wisdom of Snoopy* was part of set including *Lucy Looks at Life*, *Charlie Brown's Reflections*, and *The Meditations of Linus*. They came in a cardboard case. $30-40 set or $10-15 each. Thoughtfulness Library.

Snoopy: Everyone's Favorite Beagle Since 1950, by Charles M. Schulz, an anniversary book. $40-50

Snoopy and "It Was a Dark and Stormy Night" story book by Charles M. Schulz. Hardback with dust cover. Holt, Rinehart & Winston. Early 1970s. $15-20

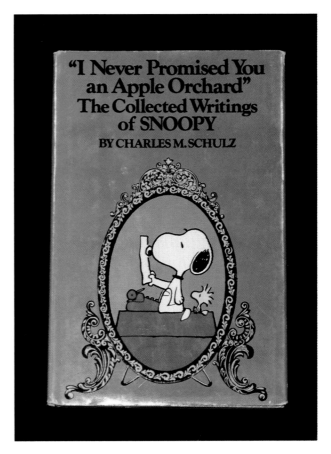

"I Never Promised You an Apple Orchard" The Collected Writings of Snoopy by Charles M. Schulz. Hardback with dust cover, story book. Holt, Rinehart & Winston. 1976. $15-20

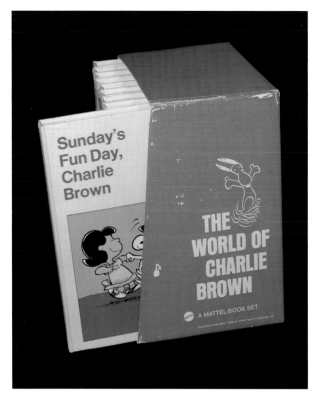

The World of Charlie Brown. "A Mattel Book Set." 1980s. $30-40

The Snoopy Collection: One Thousand Fabulous Snoopy Products.
Edited by J.C. Saures. 1982. Hardback $35-50; paperback $15-20

Charles M. Schulz: 40 Years of life and Art, by Giovanni Trinboli. Pharos
Books, New York, printed in Italy. 1990. $100-125 mint in box

Snoopy Around the World: Dressed by Top Fashion Designers.
Published by Harry Abrams, Inc. 1990. $40-60

Snoopy Et La S' Valentin. French. Dargaud. $15-20

Incroyable Snoopy. French book. Dargaud. $15-20

The Snoopy Festival, by Charles M. Schulz. Holt, Rinehart & Winston. 1974. Paperback $15-20. Hardback $30-40

Snoopy coloring book from Kuwait. Mid-1990s. $10-15

Snoopy, Come Home by Charles M. Schulz in English and Spanish versions. Holt/Rinehart/Winston Publishers. 1960s. $30-40 together..

Snoopy books in German. Paperback. Kruger. 1990s. $15-20

Snoopy Patineur. French book. Dargaud. $20-25

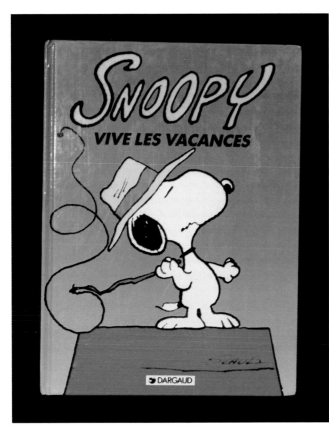

Snoopy Vive Les Vacances. French hardback book. Dargaud.
1990s. $20-25

"I Love Snoopy" Sticker Album by Panini.
Book and stickers bought indivually. 1986.
$75-100 mint book with stickers complete.

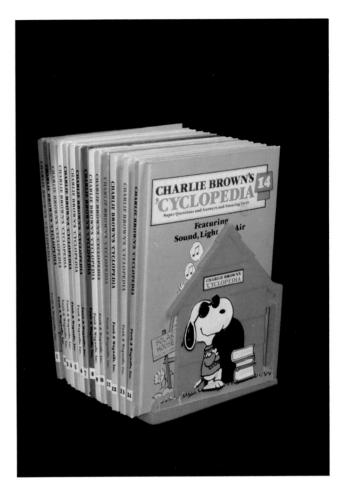

Charlie Brown's 'Cyclopedia with rack. Funk and Wagnalls. 1990s. $30-40 set with rack. 14 volumes

Peanuts Punch-out Puppet Show. Scholastic. 1980s. $12-20. "Snoopy Disguise Kit" came in other varieties.

STUFF TO DO

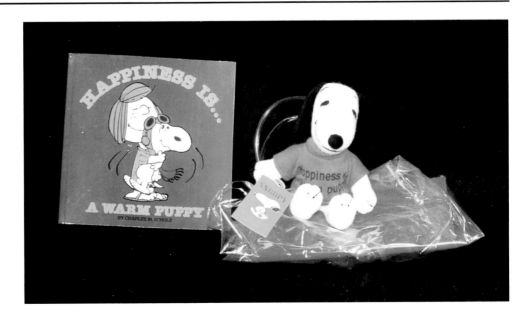

Gift pack. Book, cotton Snoopy, tote bag. Applause. Late 1980s. $15-20

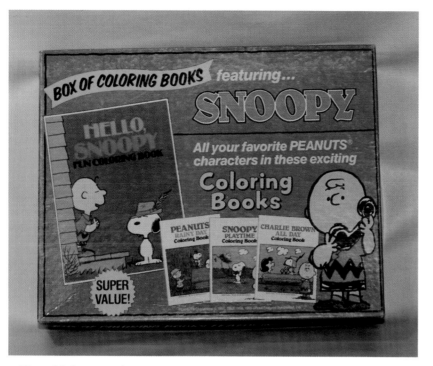

"Box of Coloring Books." Set of four by Modern Publications. 1980s. $15-20

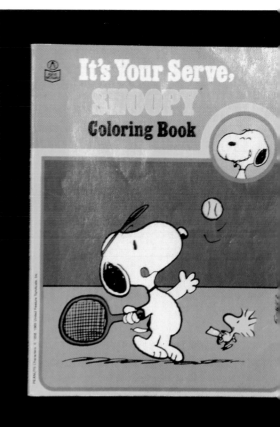

It's Your Serve, Snoopy Coloring Book. Rand McNally. 1980. $6-8

Snoopy "Posters Pen Set." Craft House Co. 1980s. $10-15

Peanuts, Sound Story musical story book. Sight and Sound Inc. 1989. $20-25

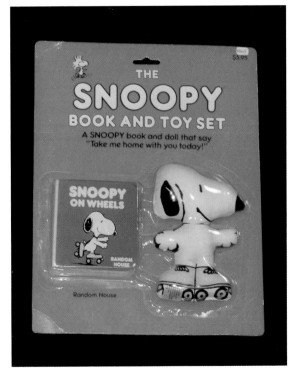

Snoopy "Busy Day" and "Fun Time" coloring books. Ottenheimer Publishers. Early 1980s. $3-5 each

Plastic "Snoopy Book and Toy Set." Random House. 1980s. $9-12

Pet Snoopy story book. Determined. 1983. $10-12 mint

Gift pack. Book, cotton Snoopy, tote bag. Applause. Late 1980s. $15-20

SIGN HERE PLEASE!

Hallmark photo album. 6" x 4.5". 1980s. $15-20

Autograph book with Snoopy carrying hobo pack. Hallmark. Early 1970s. $25-30

"Sign In Please!" Snoopy autograph book. Hallmark. 1990s. $10-15

"No Snooping" diary with lock. Hallmark. Mid-1990s. $10-15

"Super" Snoopy scrapbook. Hallmark. 1990s. $25-35

Small photo album from Knott's Berry Farm. 1980s/1990s. $10-15

Spiral Snoopy and Woodstock scrapbook album. Hallmark. Late 1970s. $25-35 mint in box

Small photo album with Snoopy puffing hot air balloon. Japan. Knotts Berry Farm. 1990s. $10-15

Snoopy photo album. Japan. Full size. 1990s. $30-40

The Peanuts gang photo album. Ambassador. 1995. $10-15

"The Peanuts Thoughtfulness Album." Hallmark. Loose leaf folders and calendar. 8" x 10". Early 1970s. $40-50

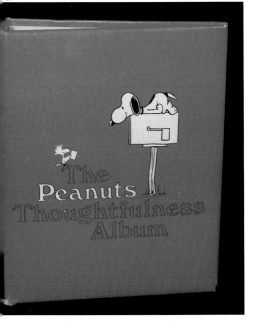

Snoopy autograph book. Hallmark. 1980s. $15-20

Snoopy Fan Club papers. 1983. $7-10 set

Booklet for 1961 Falcon with Snoopy at bottom. $35-45

Japanese advertising for ski resorts. 1990s. $6-8 each

Official program from the 85th Tournament of Roses. 1974. $15-20

Beagle Bugle newsletter, September, 1983, $15-20. The *Beagle Bugle* newsletter was published quarterly for members of the original Snoopy fan club. General manager, George Pipal and publisher, R.A. Nelson, worked out of Schulz's headquarters, 9 Snoopy Place, Santa Rosa, California. This wonderful paper was first published February, 1983 and included articles about Snoopy and the Gang, advice to pet owners, color photos from fans worldwide, new products and special offers to members for great memorabilia. Mid-1985 saw the end of the newsletter, due to the high costs of color printing and postal costs. Subscription costs were $3 for four newsletters.

Beagle Bugle newsletter. December. 1983. $15-20

Snoopy Magazine. Summer, 1988. $10-15

Snoopy Magazine, Spring Issue No. 2. 1988. $10-15. Welsh Publishing Group Inc. published *Snoopy Magazine* quarterly. It included stories, coloring pages, puzzles, riddles and even more great features. Parents could enjoy helpful tips on the parents pages in every issue. The magazine was designed for pre-schoolers and their parents, but any collector would savor every word and picture on each and every one of the 32-40 pages. A subscription was reasonably priced at $7 per year. The high cost of producing the high quality, full color magazine proved to be prohibitive. The Snoopy Magazine was published much too briefly.

Snoopy Magazine. Fall, 1988. $10-15

Snoopy Magazine, Premier Issue. Winter, 1988. $12-20

Snoopy Magazine. Summer, 1989. $10-15

Snoopy Magazine. Spring, 1990. $10-15

Snoopy Magazine. Fall, 1989. $10-15

Snoopy Magazine. Spring, 1989. $10-15

Snoopy Magazine. Winter, 1990. $10-15

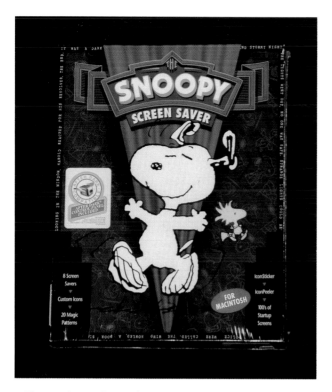

"Snoopy Screen Saver" for computer. 1990s. $20-25

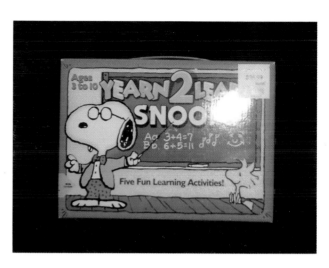

"Yearn 2 Learn" game pack software. Image Smith Inc. 1990s. $35-50 each

"Yearn 2 Learn." Contains five activity software programs. Image Smith Inc. 1990s. $35-50

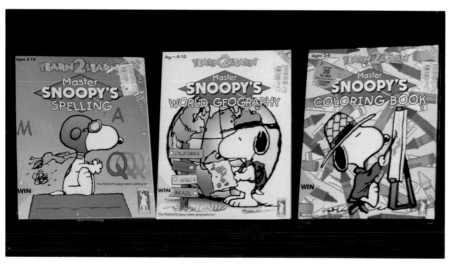

"Yearn 2 Learn" activity software. Image Smith Inc. 1990s. $20-25

Snoopy "Yearn 2 Learn" and "Snoopy's Game Club" computer software. Left: Image Smith Inc. 1990s. $20-25; right: Accolade, 1990s. $20-25 each

SNOOPY'S WARDROBE AND ACCESSORIES

WHAT TO WEAR?

Denim Snoopy child's vest. 1980s. $5-8

Cotton sailor shirt. J.G. Hook. Late 1980s-early 1990s. $25-35

Knit sweater with Snoopy skating in the snow. Design on front only. Bill Ditford. 1992. No longer made. $125-150

Knit Snoopy tennis sweater. 1980s. $60-70

Knit sweater with Snoopy as Christopher Columbus, commemorating the 500th anniversary of the discovery of America. Design on front and back. Bill Ditford design. 1992. No longer made. $185-225

Knit sweater with Snoopy giving flowers to Woodstock. "Snoopy and Friends." Mid-1990s. $25-35

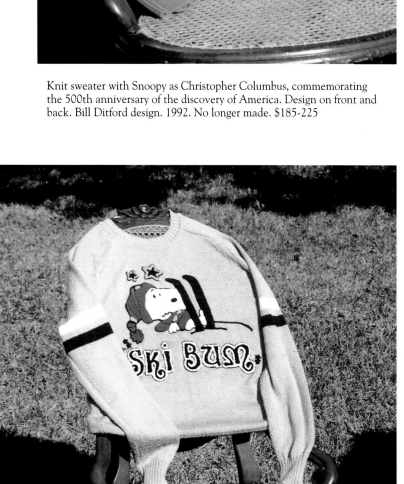

Knit sweater, "Ski Bum." Devo Inc. 1980s. $60-70

Snoopy adult's Arrow sweater, acrylic. Late 1970s. $40-50

Cotton, sequinned Snoopy sailor shirt. Marisa. Early 1990s. $90-120

Cotton Snoopy sweat shirt. French slogan reads "I'm allergic to morning." 1980s. $25-35

Genus blue jean jacket. 1995-96. Genus lost its license for Peanuts products in 1996. $200-250

I'M VERY COLD!

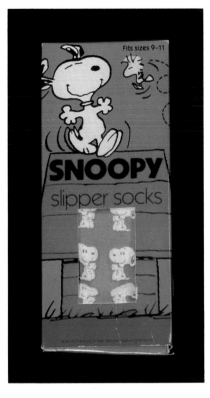

Box of "Snoopy Slipper Socks." 1990s. $5-7

Quilted jacket. 1990s. $30-40. Featured at Camp Snoopy, Knotts Berry farm.

Plush Snoopy children's slippers. 1990s. $10-15

Plush Snoopy earmuffs. 1980s/90s. $10-15

Marshmallow Snoopy head slippers. 1990s. $20-25

Rubber swim sandals. 1980s. $4-6

Rubber rain boots. 1980s. $12-15 mint

Rubber "Snoopers" rain boots. 1980s. $12-15 mint

Rubber red rain boots. 1980s. $12-15 mint

Child's acrylic socks with applique and embroidered Snoopy on doghouse. Early 1990s. Harlequin Designs. $10-15

Knit hat and knit socks, gift boxed. Accessory Network. Mid-1990s. $10-15 each.

Men's acrylic Santa Snoopy socks. 1990s. High Point Knitting Inc. $10-15

Men's acrylic Snoopy Halloween socks. 1990s. High Point Knitting Inc. $10-15

Acrylic stretch "Peanuts Magic Gloves." 1990s. $5-7

Acrylic Snoopy socks. Through the 1990s High Point Knitting Inc. made many patterns of wonderful socks for children, women and men. $4-6.

Ties. Black and white polyester tie by Cervantes, 1980s. $20-30. Maroon silk tie, 1990s. $20-30

Silk and knit Snoopy golf ties. Mid-1990s. Silk $20-30-Knit $10-15

"Snoopy Mitten Clips" from Butterfly. 1980s. $5-7

Snoopy scarf. Vera. 1990s. Discontinued in 1996. $15-20

Snoopy scarf. Cotton polyester. 1980s. $7-10

Snoopy and Woodstock scarf. Vera. 1990s. Discontinued in 1996. $15-20

Scout Snoopy cotton polyester neck scarf. 1980s. $7-10

Cotton Snoopy and Woodstock, child's handkerchief from Japan. Hallmark. 1990s. $15-20

Cotton Snoopy child's handkerchief from Japan. Hallmark. 1990s. $15-20

"Team Snoopy Wet Suit." 1990s. $25-35

Flying Ace, plastic head, "Bow Biters." Brookside. 1980. $3-5 set (no package).

"Bow Biters" by Brookside Plastic Corp. 1990s. $5-7

Shoe lace decorations. Flying Ace. Brookside. Woodstock. 1990s. $5-7

Cotton adult tee shirt. "Rainy Days in London". Blues. 1980s. $25-35

BELTS

Elastic Snoopy child's belt. 1980s. $4-6

Gift boxed wallet and key chain and scarf set. Accessory Network. Mid-1990s. $10-15 each.

Snoopy belt buckles from Oden, Inc. Embossed leather with metal base. 1980s. $15-25 each.

Elastic Snoopy child's suspenders. Lee Co. 1980s. $10-15

Elastic children's belts with plastic buckles. 1980s. $10-15 set with box

"Snoopy Patch L.A. 84" fabric Olympic patches. Determined Productions. $7-12 each

Snoopy and Peanuts patterns from Simplicity. 1980s. $12-18

"Snoopy" and "Belle" "Patch L.A. 84" fabric Olympic patches. Determined. $7-12 each

Plastic buttons from JHB International. Early 1990s. $3-5 each package

"Snoopy Patch L.A. 84" washable/iron on/sew on fabric patches. Commemorating the 1984 Olympics in Los Angeles. 12 varieties available. Determined. $7-12 each

Fabric Snoopy sports patches. Early 1970s. Determined. Matches pillows stuffed with Kapok. 3". $7-12 each

Plastic Snoopy umbrella. 1990s. $10-15

Plastic child's Snoopy umbrella. 1990s. $10-15

Nylon child's umbrella, Peanuts
Gang. Shaw Creations.1990s. $10-15

Snoopy and Joe Cool plastic sun glasses. Right: Mid-1990s. Metal $7-12. Left: 1980s-1990s. Plastic. $3-6

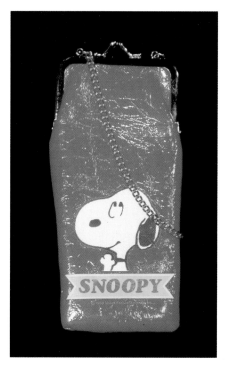

Vinyl eye glass case on chain. Snoopy on front. $15-20

Vinyl eye glass cases. $15-20 each

Vinyl eye glass cases. $15-20 each

Snoopy vinyl eye glass case. $15-20

SNOOPY TO GO: PURSES, TOTES, AND TRAVEL BAGS

Snoopy coin purses. Various makers including Hallmark. 1980s. $6-10 each

Vinyl wallets. Early 1980s. $12-15 each

Snoopy wallets. Variety of makers including Quantasia, Butterfly and Aviva. 1980s-90s. $8-20 each

Canvas mini Snoopy bag. 1980s. $3-6

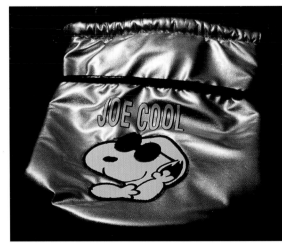

Silver Lamé bag. China. Late 1990s. Can hang by suction cups on strap. $15-20

Canvas Snoopy purse. 1970s. $12-18

Fabric carry-all bag. 1980s. $12-18

Canvas Snoopy "Love" tote bag. 1970s. $12-18

Canvas Snoopy tote bag. Determined. 1980s. $10-15

Fabric Christmas Snoopy purse. Horizon Designs. Mid-1990s. $10-12

Vinyl tote bag. "Snoopy's Astro Bag." Natco Products Corp. 1969. $25-35

Fabric carry-all bag. Butterfly. Late 1970s-1980s. $7-12

Fabric carry all bag. 1990s. $10-15

Fabric Snoopy tote bag. Cut and sew fabric. 1970s. $8-12

Plastic see-thru carry-all bag. Phoenix Corp. Ltd. Japan. 1990s. $10-15

Plastic Scout Snoopy and Woodstock bag. Phoenix Corp. Ltd. Japan. 1990s. $10-15

Plastic see-thru carry-all bag. Sanrio. Japan. 1990s. $10-15

Plastic Snoopy tote bags. Sanrio,1990s. Japan. $10-15 each

Fabric Snoopy sports bag. 1980s. $15-20

Fabric carry-all bag. Horizon Kids. Early 1990s. $12-20

Fabric Christmas overnight/duffle bag.
Horizon Designs. Mid-1990s. $15-20

Vinyl Snoopy head purse.
Jaclyn Inc. 1996. $15-20

Fabric Christmas Snoopy purse. Horizon
Designs. Mid-1990s. $10-12

Fabric back pack. Accessory Network. 1990s.
$15-20

Plastic Snoopy and Woodstock
duffle bag. Accessory Network.
1990s. $15-20

Fabric swim bag. Butterfly. 1980s. $15-20
mint

Fabric beach bag. Butterfly. 1980s. $15-20

Fabric beach bag. Butterfly. 1980s.
$15-20

Fabric beach bag. Horizon Kids.
1990s. $15-20

Nylon "Jets" sports bag.
Quantasia. 1980s. $15-20

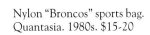

Nylon "Giants" sports bag.
Quantasia. 1980s. $15-20

Nylon "Broncos" sports bag.
Quantasia. 1980s. $15-20

Nylon "Chiefs" sports bag.
Quantasia. 1980s. $15-20
Quantasia made a variety of
products with different teams
including wallets, large duffles,
roll bags, and more.

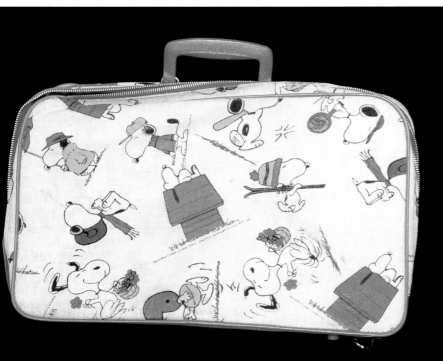

Canvas suitcase. Armored Luggage Mfg. Co. 1970s. $25-35

Canvas suitcase. Aviva. 1980s. $30-40

Vinyl suitcase. Quantasia. 1980s. $40-50

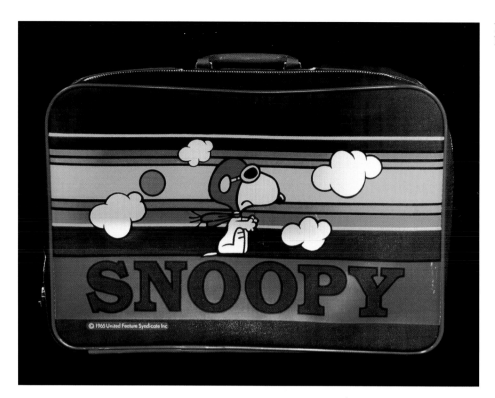

Fabric suitcase from Aviva. Flying Ace. Early 1980s. $30-40

Vinyl Snoopy suitcase. 1990s. Came in two sizes. $40-60

Snoopy World Tour #1 carrying case. 12"x8"x11". $20-30

SNOOPY'S HOLIDAY

VALENTINE'S DAY

Cotton Snoopys. Applause valentine selection. 1990s. $6-8 each

Cardboard valentine centerpiece from Hallmark. 1980s. $15-20 mint

Snoopy snack canisters. Sold with cheese or caramel popcorn. 1980s. $7-9 each

Valentine's day greeting card. Hallmark. 1990s. $2-3

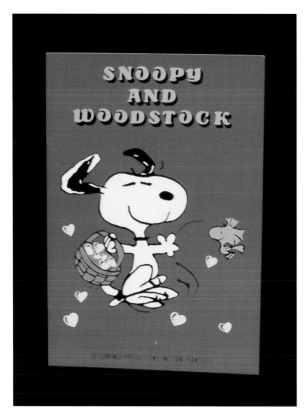

Dancing Snoopy and Woodstock booklet. 1990s. Japan. $4-6

"Snoopy Valentines" in doghouse box, from Hallmark. 1970s. $20-30 complete.

"Peanuts Valentines" in doghouse box, from Hallmark. 1970s. $20-30 complete.

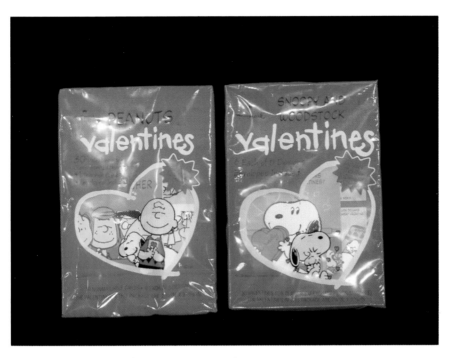

Packages of valentines from Hallmark. 1990s. $3-5 each.

Sweetheart greeting card. Hallmark. 1980s. $4-5

"Snoopy and Woodstock" valentines. Ambassador. 1990s. $3-5

Ceramic love coffee cups. $8-15 each

Variety of Valentine refrigerator magnets. Mid-1990s. Magnetic Collectibles Inc. $3-4 each

Valentine candy with Snoopy or Woodstock fun figure on front from Whitman's. Mid-1990s. $3-4 each.

ST. PAT'S DAY

Cotton St. Patrick's Day Snoopy rag dolls. 4.5". Applause. 1991. $6-8 each

Plastic St. Patrick's Day pin from Hallmark. 1996. $3-4

THE EASTER BEAGLE IS COMING!

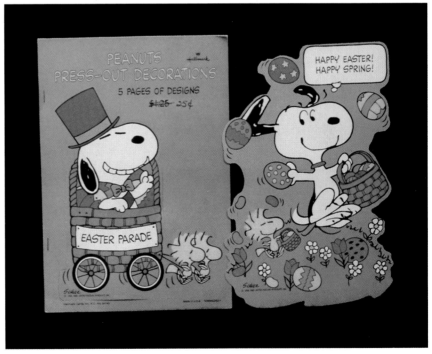

Easter "Peanuts Press-out Decorations" from Hallmark. 1970s. $15-20 mint

Cardboard Easter basket. Hallmark. Early 1980s. $5-7

Resin Easter "Keepsake Ornaments." Hallmark. 1995-1996. 1994 not pictured. $15-20 each w/box.

Mylar balloon on a stick. 1980s/90s. $2-3

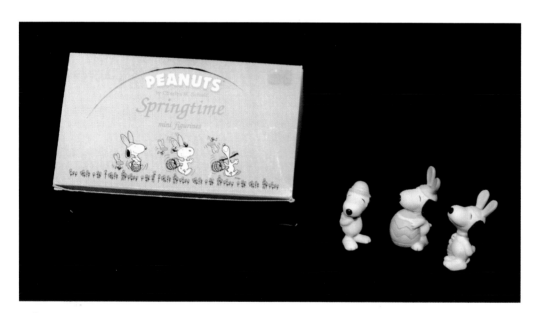

Ceramic "Springtime Mini Figurines." Snoopy in different poses. Willitts. 1990. $30-35 set

Snoopy figurine with "Happy Easter" balloon from Willitts. 1990. $15-20

Hallmark Easter Snoopy pin. Hallmark. 1995. $3-4

Plush Easter Beagle. Determined. Late 1980s. $15-20

Ceramic Easter egg ornament. Napkin ring base not included. Willitts. 1990. $10-15

Tricot Easter Beagles. Came in small Whitman's Easter baskets. 1995. $4-6 each.

"It's the Easter Beagle Charlie Brown" VHS video. 1974. $10-12

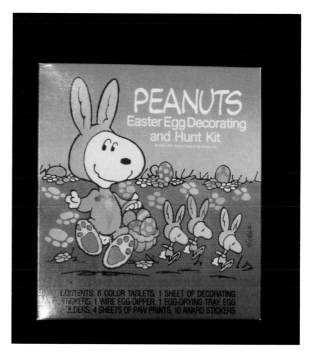

Easter egg decorating kit. Hallmark. Early 1990s. $4-6

Easter egg with bubble gum inside. Leaf Co. Mid-1990s. $2-3

Easter candy with Snoopy or Woodstock fun figure on front from Whitman's. Mid-1990s. $3-4 each.

Plastic Easter egg banks filled with candy from Whitman's. 1996. $6-10

Large Easter basket from Whitman's Chocolate Co. Mid-1990s. $15-20

Small Easter basket from Whitman's Chocolate Co. Mid-1990s. $8-10

Snoopy as Easter Beagle, egg wraps. (Place egg, in wrap, into boiling water. It then shrinks to fit egg perfectly.) Hallmark. 1980s. $7-10 per dozen

"Snoopy and Peanuts Gang Egg Decorating Kit." Easter Unlimited. Late 1980s. $4-6

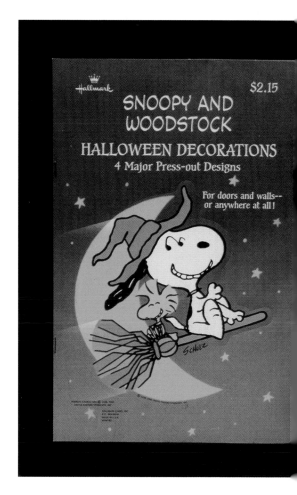

Paper plates, cups, napkins, table cover. Halloween collection. Hallmark. 1990s. $4-11 each.

Plastic Halloween decoration. Flashing light. Packaged in colorful bag. Hallmark. Early 1990s. $10-15 mint.

"Snoopy and Woodstock Halloween Decorations" from Hallmark. Early 1990s. $4-6

Snoopy Halloween invitations from Hallmark. Early 1990s. $4-6

"Snoopy Pumpkin Cutter." Early 1990s. $5-15 w/package.

Dracula Snoopy Halloween decoration. Hallmark. 1980s. $3-4

Halloween Snoopy fun figures with boxed candy from Whitman's. 1995. $2-3

Halloween decoration, Snoopy in mask and cape. Hallmark. 1990s. $2-3

Halloween candy from Whitman's. Mid-1990s. $1-2

Plastic Halloween mask. Accompanied inexpensive vinyl children's costume. 1980s-90s. $5-8 mask alone

Rubber Snoopy children's mask. Topstone Industries. 1994. $10-15

Plastic Snoopy Halloween costume with mask. Collegeville Costumes. 1980s. $15-30 in box.

Plastic Flying Ace adult mask. 1990s. $60-75

TURKEY TIME

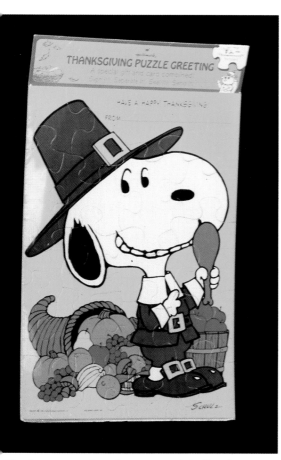

Thanksgiving puzzle and greeting card. Hallmark. 1980s. $8-12

A Charlie Brown Thanksgiving story book. Paperback. Scholastic. 1970s. $4-6

Thanksgiving card, with Snoopy as a pilgrim. Hallmark. 1980s. 12" $3-4. 3 foot version. $10-15.

Thanksgiving decoration with Snoopy eating turkey leg. Hallmark. 1980s. $3-4

Willitts Christmas votive candle holder. Late1980s. $20-30

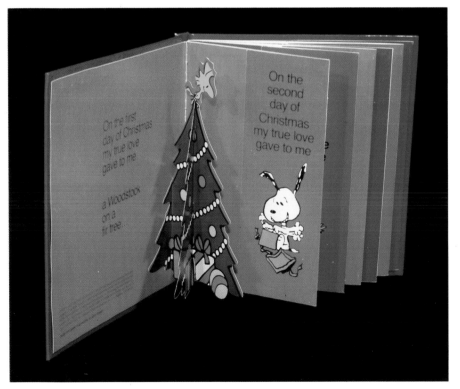

Snoopy and the Twelve Days of Christmas, pop up book. Inside view. Determined. 1980s. $20-30

Crocheted Snoopy ornament. Determined. 1980s. $15-30 w/package

Silver-tone Christmas ornament. Determined. 1980s. $15-20

Gold-tone Christmas ornament. Determined. 1980s. $15-20

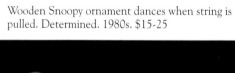

Wooden Snoopy ornament dances when string is pulled. Determined. 1980s. $15-25

Snoopy satin Christmas ornament. Doghouse-shaped box. Hallmark. 1978. $20-25

Ceramic Snoopy with Christmas tree by Determined Productions. 2.75". 1975. $20-30

"Snoopy and friends Satin Christmas Ornament." Determined Productions. 1980s. $15-20

Ceramic Snoopy on present ornament. Determined Productions. 1970s. $20-30

Ceramic English Snoopy, ornament, Determined 3". 1977. $25-40. Other in the International Series but not pictured: Mexico, Snoopy in sombrero; Germany, Tyrolene outfit; Spain, bullfighting outfit; England, palace guard outfit; Scandanavia, with viking helmet; Japan, wearing kimono; Transylvania, cape and top hat. $25-40 each.

Ceramic Snoopy with candy cane by Determined Productions. 2.25". 1975. $20-30

Ceramic Snoopy playing cello by Determined Prod. 1976. 2.5". $25-40 Other in the Musician Series, but not pictured: Peppermint Patty playing guitar; Linus playing tenor sax; Charlie Brown playing bass drum; and Lucy playing trumpet. $25-40 each.

Flat ceramic ornament from Determined Productions, 1978. 3". $25-40. Others in set but not shown are: Woodstock on package; Snoopy leaping with candy cane; Snoopy carrying Woodstock atop a package; and Snoopy wearing red and green stripped stocking hat. In another set not pictured from Determined Productions, 1980 are: Snoopy lying on wreath; Woodstock on Noel; Snoopy carrying Christmas tree; Snoopy angel; Santa Snoopy going down chimney; and Woodstock angel. $25-40 each

Ceramic Snoopy holding wreath, ornament by Determined Productions. 1975. $25-40

Ceramic Snoopy Scottish bagpipe player, ornament. International Series. Determined Productions, 1977. $25-40

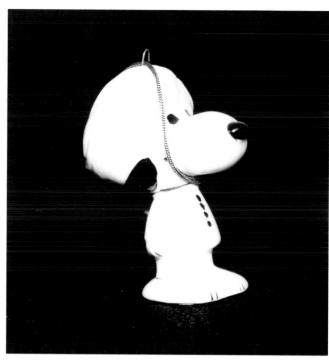

Ceramic India Snoopy ornament, by Determined Productions. International Series. 3". 1977. $25-40

Ceramic Italian Snoopy from International Series by Determined. 1977. $25-40

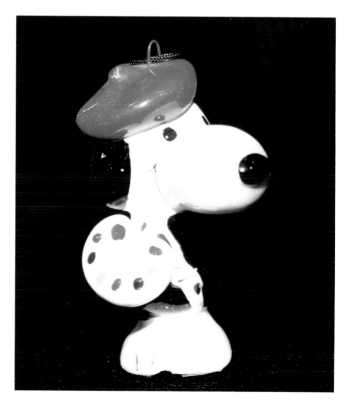

Ceramic French Snoopy artist from International Series by Determined. 1977. $25-40

Plastic Snoopy in blue race car ornament. 1980s. $5-7.

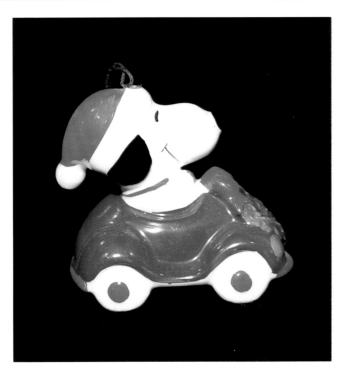

Ceramic Snoopy Santa in car ornament. Vehicle Series by Determined Products. 2.5". 1979. $25-40

Ceramic Snoopy in boat with tree, ornament. Vehicle Series. 2.5". 1979. $25-40. Others from the Vehicle Series but not shown: Santa Woodstock in firetruck and Santa Snoopy in steam engine. $25-40 each

Ceramic Flying Ace Snoopy ornament, from Vehicle Series by Determined Productions. 1979. $25-40

Snoopy ceramic ornament. Determined. 1980s. $20-30 w/box.

Ceramic Snoopy detective ornament from Adventure Series. By Determined Products. 1975. 2.75". Others in the series but not shown: Clown, Robin hood, Davy Crockett, Indian, Bandit. $25-40 each.

Willitts miniature snowball Snoopy ornament. Early 1990s. $20-30

"Snoopy and Friends" Christmas ornament. 3-D plastic Panorama in globe style ornament. Dated and limited editions. 5 in the series. Hallmark. 1982. $75-100. The Series included: 1979, "Ice Hockey Holiday," $150-200; 1980, "Ski Holiday," $100-125; 1981, "Snoopy and Friends" (Snoopy rides in sleigh past snowman shaped like Snoopy), $75-100; 1982, "Snoopy and Friends" as shown; 1983, "Santa Snoopy," $60-90

Willitts various ceramic Christmas ornaments. 1980s-90s. $20-30 each w/box.

Porcelain ornament, Snoopy riding carousel horse. Willitts. Late 1980s. $25-40 w/box.

Porcelain disc ornament from Willitts. Snoopy on doghouse, 1990. $15-30 w/box.

Porcelain disc ornament with Snoopy, Charlie Brown, and Woodstock from Willitts. 1990. $15-30 w/box.

Ceramic micro mini bells. 1" x 1". "Genuine bone china, Taiwan". Early 1980s. $15-20. Not pictured: Snoopy lying on dog house; Charlie Brown eating candy cane; Snoopy opening gifts; Santa Snoopy giving Lucy gift; Snoopy holds Woodstock with decorated nest. $15-20 each.

Ceramic Christmas bell ornament. One of a series. 1980s. $25-40

Ceramic Christmas bell. 1977. Schmid. $30-45 w/box.

Willitts porcelain Christmas ornament. 1989. $15-25 in box

Ceramic Christmas bell. Schmid. 1975. $30-45 w/box.

Plastic "Stocking Hanger." Hallmark. Early 1980s. $30-45

Snoopy with gift and Woodstock sitting on gift mini candles. Hallmark, 1990s.. $5-8 each

Acrylic non-woven Snoopy caroler Christmas tree skirt. 1993. Holiday Products. $10-15

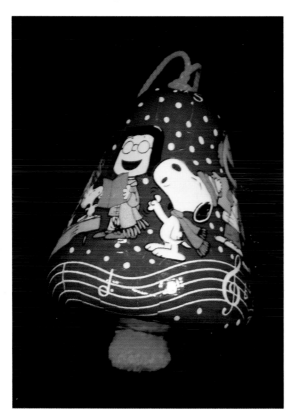

Styrafoam Christmas ornament. 1980s. $10-20

Fleece Santa Snoopy Christmas stocking. 1980s. $15-20

Cotton Snoopy Christmas stocking. Determined. 1980s. $15-25, 18" size; $8-15, 6" size.

Acrylic knit Snoopy Christmas stocking. 1980s. $15-20

Cotton Snoopy Christmas stocking. 1980s. $15-25

Acrylic non-woven Christmas stocking. Holiday Products. 16". 1993. $4-6 each

Acrylic non-woven Christmas stockings. Holiday Products. 16". 1993. $4-6 each.

Acrylic non-woven mini Christmas stockings. Holiday Products. 1993. $4-6 set

Party Christmas coasters from Hallmark. 1980s. $7-10

"Holiday Card Assortment" from Hallmark. 1990s. $10-15

Box of Snoopy Christmas cards. Hallmark. Mid-1990s. $15-20

Package of "Christmas Cards for Kids." Hallmark. 1990s. $4-6

Paper, Christmas placemat from Hallmark. 1970s. $3-5 each

Cardboard Christmas puzzle. Hallmark. 1980s. $8-12

Holiday greeting puzzle from Hallmark. 1980s. $8-12

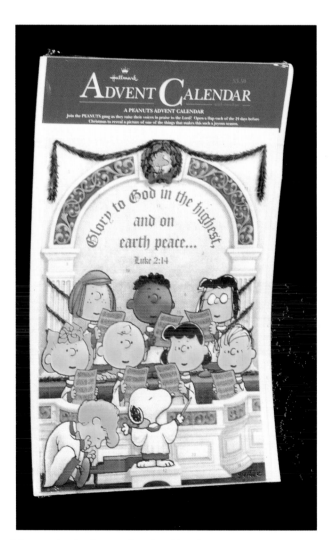

Advent calendar from Hallmark. 1990s. $5-7

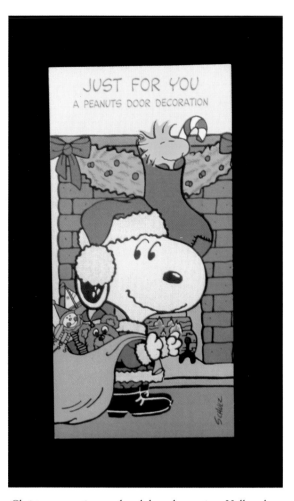

Christmas greeting card and door decoration. Hallmark.
1990s. $4-5

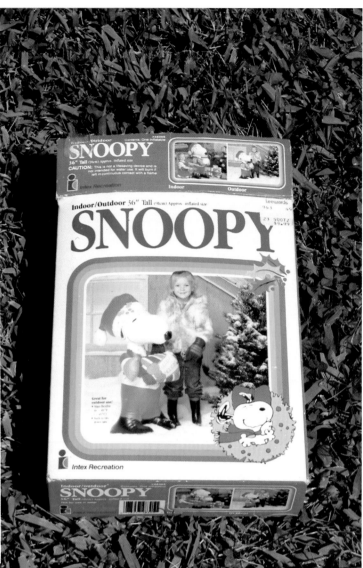

Inflatable Christmas Snoopy Santa for outdoors. Intex. Late
1980s. $15-25

Tin Snoopy Christmas tray. Willitts.
1990. $15-25

Cotton Christmas pot holders. 1990s. Cannon. $4-7 each

Terry cloth Christmas towels.
Cannon. 1990s. $5-10 each

Ceramic Macy's Parade 1987 coffee cup.
$12-20 each

Holiday towel and oven mit set. Barth and
Dreyfuss. 1990s. $10-20 set

Ceramic Christmas coffee cups. Willitts.
1990s. $10-15 each

Ceramic Christmas coffee cups. Determined.
1980s. $12-20 each

Ceramic Christmas cups. "Cool Yule." Willitts. Late
1980s, early 1990s. $30-45 set w/box.

Cotton Snoopy Christmas
carry-all. Horizon Kids. 1994.
$15-20

Cotton Christmas apron with
cookie cutters. Horizon Designs.
Mid-1990s. $15-20

Plastic holiday waste basket. Saturday
Knight Ltd. 1990s. $20-30

Fabric Christmas purses. Horizon
Kids. 1994. $12-15 each

"3-Piece Bath Set." Saturday Knight Ltd. 1990s. $15-20

Christmas Snoopy cardboard display. 1990s. $10-15

Christmas Snoopy throw rug. Saturday Knight Ltd. Early 1990s. $20-35

Christmas plastic bathroom set. Saturday Knight Ltd. 1990s. $15-20

Christmas welcome mat, indoor or outdoor. Bacova Guild Ltd. Olefin Carpets. 1990s. $10-15

Christmas Snoopy ornaments with boxed candy from Whitman's. 1995. $4-5 each

Christmas door mat. "And a beagle in a pear tree." Bacova Guild Ltd. Olefin carpets. 1990s. $10-15

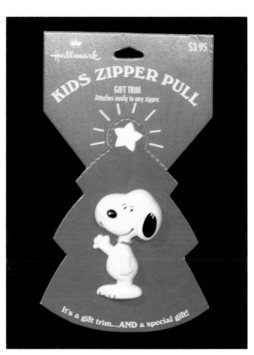

"Kids Zipper Pull" from Hallmark. 1995. $4-6

Christmas ornaments on box of Whitman's Chocolates. 1995. $4-5 each

Inflatable plastic Christmas baby ball, 1990s. Child's Guidance/Remco. $3-4

PARTY TIME

Snoopy and the Red Baron centerpiece from Hallmark. 1970s. $20-25

"Party Door Decoration" from Hallmark. 1990s. $5-7

Cardboard Snoopy tiny gift box. Hallmark. 1980s-90s. $2-3

Plastic "Snoopy Party Picks" from Hallmark. 1970s. $8-12

LET'S GO SWIMMING

Nylon infant's life vest. Stearns Mf' g. 1990s. $20-25

Nylon toddlers life vest. Stearns
Mf' g. 1980s. $20-25

Nylon youth life vest. 1980s. $20-25

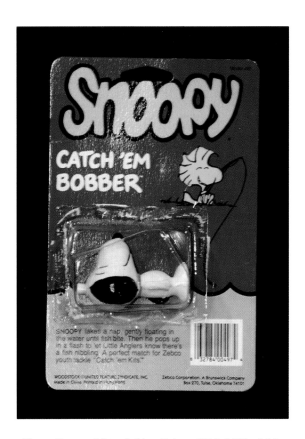

Plastic Snoopy fishing bobber. Zebco. 1980s/1990s. $5-8

Nylon "Snoopy Catch 'em" tote. Zebco. Holds tackle, bait, worms, hooks. 1990s. $5-10

Snoopy fishing pole. Zebco. 1980s/90s. $15-25

Plastic inflatable beach ball. 1990s. Japan. $5-10

Inflatable swim vest. "The Wet Set." Intex. 1990s. $5-10

Vinyl water wings. Mattel. $5-10

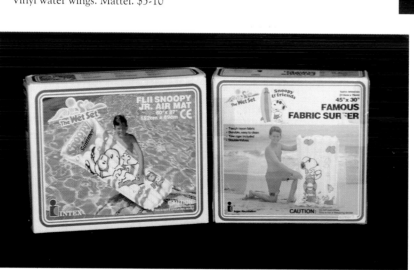

Vinyl pool toys. "The Wet Set." Intex. 1990s. Boat: $15-30. Toys: $5-10 each

Plastic inflatable air mats. "The Wet Set." Intex. 1990s. $15-25 each

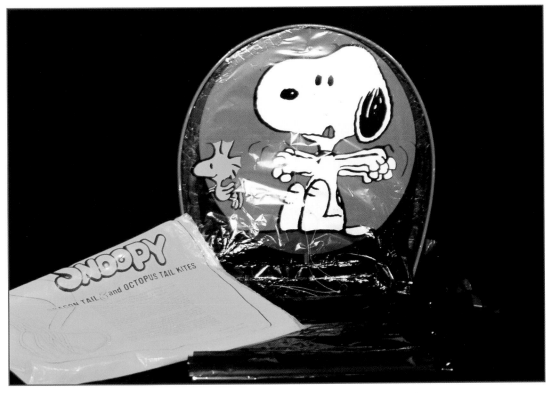

Mylar Snoopy kite. Crunden Martin Mf' g. 1980s. $10-20 w/package

Mylar Snoopy kite. 1980s. Crunden Martin Mf' g. $10-20 w/package

Plastic Snoopy kites. 1980s. Right: $6-8. Left: Met Life-free promotion. Early 1990s. $3-4

Plastic Flying Ace kite. Late 1970s. $6-10

Mylar Snoopy and Woodstock kite. Quicksilver. 1980s. $10-20

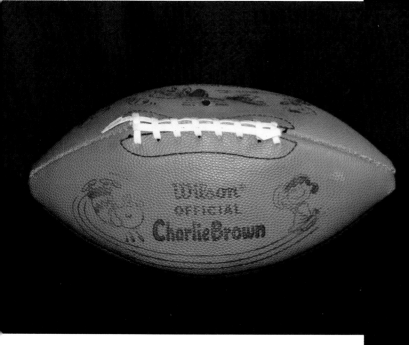

Wilson Charlie Brown leather football. 1969. $150-175

Linus mini poster. Hallmark. 1980s. $3-5

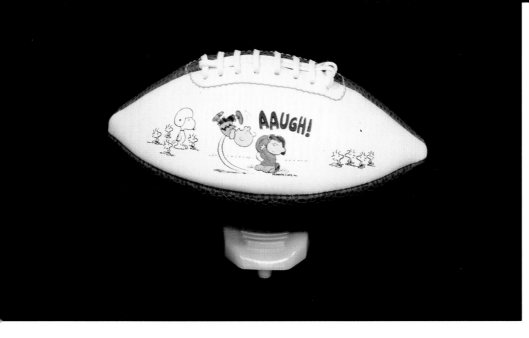

Leather-like "Fotoball" football. 1995. $20-30 boxed

Leather Snoopy "Fotoball" baseball and glove. 1995. $20-30 boxed

Plastic Peanuts baseball. Part of Playskool "Snoopy Slugger" included with oversized yellow bat and orange/white cap. Late 1970s. Ball $5-7 as is. $30-40 set

Leather Charlie Brown "Fotoball" baseball and glove. 1995. $20-30 boxed

Snoopy baseball. Hutch-soft vinyl. 1990s. $10-15

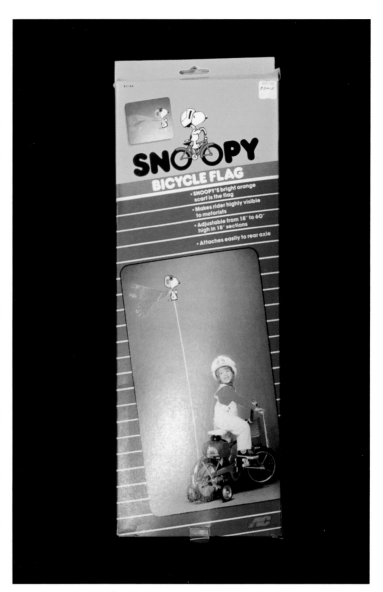

Bicycle flag with Flying Ace on end. AC International. 1980s & 1990s. $15-25

Plastic water bottle. AC International. 1980s-1990s. $5-10

Plastic bicycle baskets. 1980s-90s. $5-10 each

Handlebar toy and bicycle horn. AC International. 1980s-90s. $5-10 each

Bicycle spoke reflectors. Snoopy on bike. Hallmark. 1980s. $10-15 packaged

Plastic bike siren. AC International. 1980s & 1990s. $15-20 packaged

FAO Schwarz Snoopy Bike Rider. This toy store offered some Special Edition plushes made by Applause. 18" with outfit. Also available Belle. $75-100

Metal bicycle bells. AC International. 1980s-90s. $5-10 each

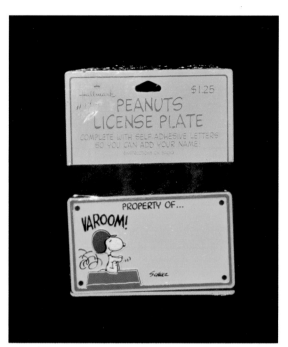

Metal Peanuts license plate from Hallmark. 1980s.
$10-15 packaged

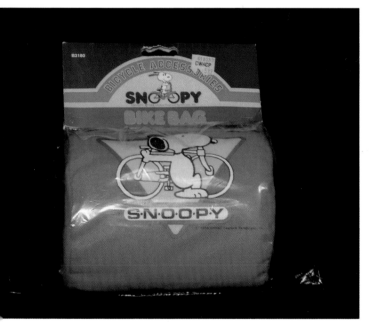

Plastic "Snoopy Bike Bag." Butterfly/Hollywood Accessories. 1980s.
$10-15

Nylon back pack. Butterfly/
Hollywood Accessories.
1980s. $15-25

SNOOPY'S MUSIC

Wooden music box. Flying Ace from Anri. 1969. $80-125

Wooden music box. Snoopy with doghouse from Anri. 1971. $125-175

Wooden music box. Snoopy on doghouse as astronaut. Schmid, 1971 $80-125

Wooden Flying Ace music box. Schmid. 1971. $100-175

Wooden Flying Ace music box. Schmid, 1973. $100-175

Musical ceramic mug, Flying Ace. Schmid. Early 1970s. $50-75

Wooden Snoopy on doghouse, music box. Woodstock carries coin inside. Schmid, 1971. $80-125

Wooden music box with drawer by Aviva. Ceramic Snoopy revolves with music. 1974. $75-100

Ceramic Snoopy skiing, music box by Aviva. 1973. $50-75

Fabric Quantasia music box. 1980s. $45-70 boxed. Others not shown: Belle in arobic pose; Snoopy on drum; Snoopy holding ball; Snoopy atop black hat; Baby Snoopy with bib and bottle. $45-70 each, boxed.

Plastic "Snoopy & Woodstock" music box. Quantasia. Mid-1980s. $30-50 boxed

Ceramic Snoopy music box. Willitts. 1990. $40-75 boxed

Ceramic Snoopy music box. Aviva. Mid-1970s. $50-75

Ceramic Snoopy atop dog house music box by Aviva. 1974. $50-75

Ceramic Flying Ace music box. Willitts. 1989. $40-75 boxed

Ceramic Snoopy caroler music box by Willitts. 1988. $45-75 boxed

Ceramic Soccer player music box made by Willitts. 1989. $40-75 boxed

Ceramic Easter Beagle music box made by Willitts. 1990. $40-75 boxed

Ceramic Christmas house music box made by Willitts. 1989. $40-75 boxed

Ceramic Santa Snoopy music box by Willitts. 1990. $40-75 boxed

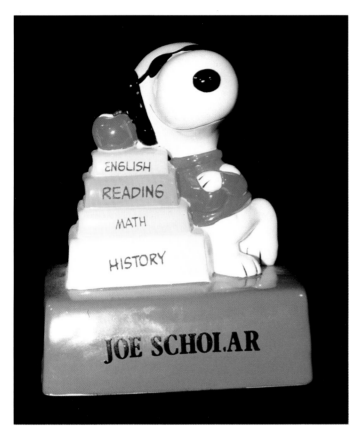

Ceramic "Joe Scholar" by Willitts. 1980. $40-75 boxed

Snoopy on musical carousel horse. Willitts. 1989. $100-175 boxed

Resin Snoopy and Woodstock music box. Willitts. Beaglefest
commemorative, very few made. 1993. $65-85

Ceramic/glass Snoopy on doghouse
Christmas glitter dome. Willitts. 1990.
$50-75 boxed

Plastic Snoopy in sleigh,
revolving snow dome.
Willitts. 1989. $40-50

Plastic Snoopy conductor in dome.
Revolving band. Willitts. 1991.
$50-75 boxed

Plastic Christmas revolving
Snoopy snow dome. Willitts.
1989. $40-50

40th Anniversary glitter dome. Ceramic/glass.
Willitts. 1990s. $50-75 boxed

TURN DOWN THAT MUSIC!

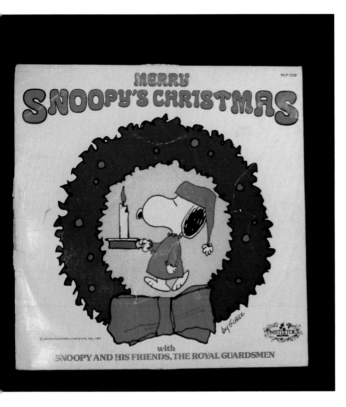

"Snoopy's Merry Christmas" LP record. Springboard International Records. 1978. $15-25

Shower radio. "Joe Cool Wet Tunes" by Salton. Early 1990s. $20-35

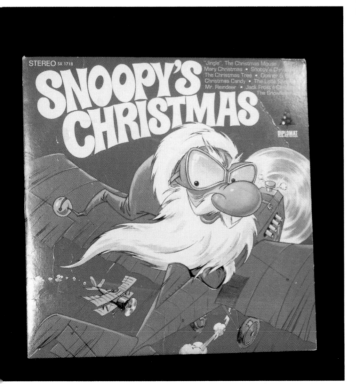

"Snoopy's Christmas" record. LP. Diplomat. 1970s. $15-25

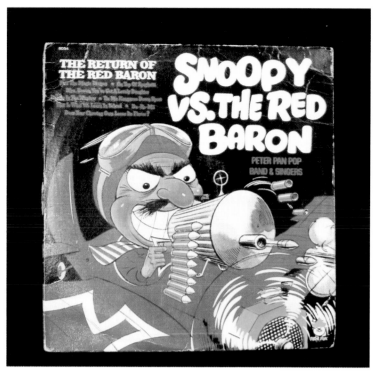

"Snoopy vs. the Red Baron" record. LP. Peter Pan Records. 1970s. $15-25

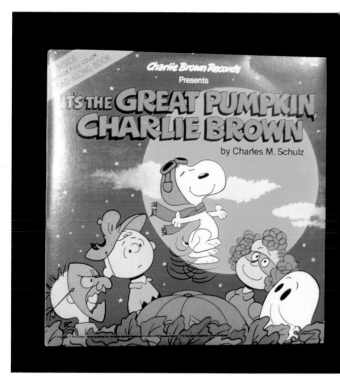

"It's the Great Pumpkin, Charlie Brown" record with book. LP. 1978. United Features Syndicate, Buena Vista Distribution. $15-25

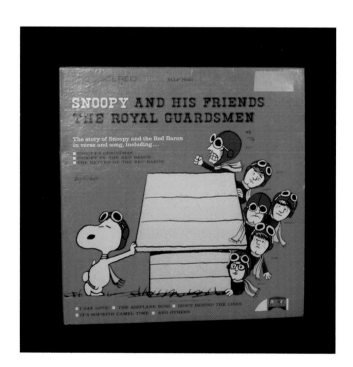

"Snoopy and His Friends the Royal Guardsmen" record. 1970s. $15-20

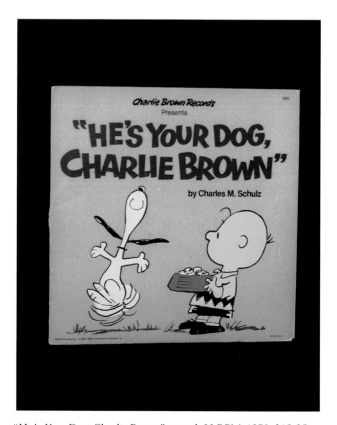

"He's Your Dog, Charlie Brown" record. 33 RPM. 1978. $15-25

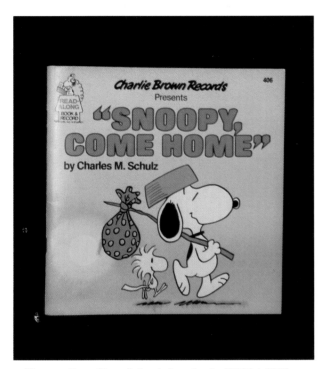

"Snoopy Come Home". Read along book. 45 RPM. 1980.
$10-15

"Snoopy's Christmas" CDs and ornaments. Mid-1990s. $15-20
each

Compact disc ornaments from CEMA. 1993. $15-20 each

"Happy Anniversary Charlie Brown" and "Snoopy's Christmas," CDs.
1995. $15-25 each

Snoopy plastic telephone. Determined Products. 1980s. $30-50 w/box

Joe Cool plastic telephone. Seika. 1990s. $75-100 w/box

Plastic Snoopy and Woodstock telephone on woodgrain base.
American Telecommunications Corp. 1980s. $150-200

Wooden candlestick lamp. Snoopy and Woodstock glass globe.
Kamco. 1978. $75-100

Plastic and woodgrain Snoopy and Woodstock lamp and telephone. American Telecommunications Corp. 1980s. $175-200

Snoopy and Woodstock lamp with rainbow. Plastic. Nursery Originals, early 1980s. $75-100

Ceramic base lamp. Snoopy holding balloons. Paper shade. Nursery Originals, early 1980s. $75-100

Ceramic lamp with Snoopy at typewriter. Metal shade. C.N. Burman. Early 1980s. $50-75 w/box

Ceramic sitting Snoopy night light. 1990. Willitts. $25-40 w/box

Plastic light up Snoopy lamp. Bulb inside. Gladys Goose Inc. 18". 1980. $60-75

Ceramic standing Snoopy lamp. C.N. Burman. Early 1980s. $50-75 w/box

Lamp with Snoopy in tux next to lamp post. Unknown manufacturer. $75-125

Snoopy catching butterflies, Japanese lantern. 1990s. $15-25

Plastic switch cover. 1980s. $6-10 without package

Plastic light switch plates. Butterfly Co., Hallmark.
Monogram Products. 1980s. $8-15 each, in package

Plastic night lights. General
Electric. 1980s-90s. $4-7
each

Plastic light switch plates. Hallmark. 1970s. $8-15 in package, $6-10 without package.

Plastic light switch plate. Wecolite. 1980s-1990s. $5-10

Plastic light switch plates. 1980s. $8-15 in package, $6-10 without package.

Snoopy ice cream maker. Donvier. 1980s. $20-35 w/box

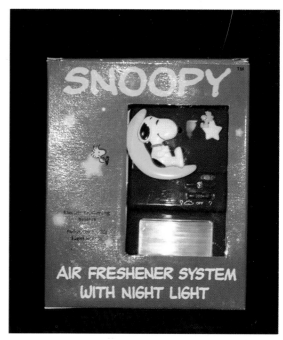

Plastic air freshener with night light. $25-40 w/box

Charlie Brown and Snoopy teflon sandwich maker from Salton. 1990s. $30-45 w/box

"Snoopy's Waffle Maker." Mid-1990s. Salton. $30-45 w/box

Plastic hair dryer from Salton. Mid-1990s. $30-45 w/box

Metal alarm clock. Snoopy dancing. Blessing/Determined. Early 1970s. 10". Came in different colors. $75-100

Metal alarm clock with Snoopy's arms as the clock hands. West Germany/Blessing/Determined Products. $35-75 w/package

Metal alarm clock. Snoopy's arms move. Was available in many color combinations. Blessing/Determined. Early 1970s. 3.5" diameter. $35-75 w/package

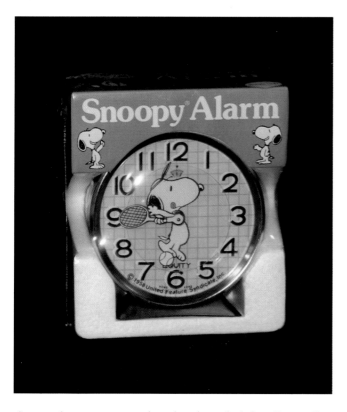

Snoopy playing tennis, metal windup alarm clock from Equity. 4". 1980s. $35-75

Snoopy and Woodstock plastic battery operated alarm clock from Equity. Early 1980s. $40-50 in box

Football playing Snoopy, metal windup alarm clock from Equity. 4". Early 1980s. $35-75

"Live It Up a Little," metal windup alarm clock from Equity. Early 1980s. 4". $35-75

Plastic clock from Citizen. 1980s.
$20-40 w/package

Metal alarm clock. "I'm allergic to morning."
4". Equity. Early 1980s. $35-75 w/package

Metal alarm clock by Equity. Snoopy with checkered flag. Early
1980s. 4". $35-75 w/package

Snoopy with Woodstock alarm clock from Citizen, Japan. 1990s.
$20-30

Plastic Snoopy wall clock. Citizen. Late 1980s. $30-40

Beagle Scout pendulum clock. Citizen, late 1980s. $50-75 w/package

Plastic goldtone clock. Japan. Late 1990s. 7". IDO Co. Ltd. $20-30

Plastic Snoopy with Woodstock clock by Citizen. 1980s. $25-40

Plush Snoopy with quartz analog alarm clock in belly. Armitron. 1990. $40-55

Joe Cool quartz alarm clock from
Salton. 1990s. $20-30

Digital alarm clock. Snoopy's doghouse by Salton.
1990s. $20-30

Plastic quartz wall clock by Salton.
1990s. $18-25

Keywound alarm clock by Salton. Metal
and Plastic. 1990s. $15-25

Plastic Snoopy with Woodstock clock.
1990s. $40-60

SNOOPY FINERY

CRYSTAL ANYONE?

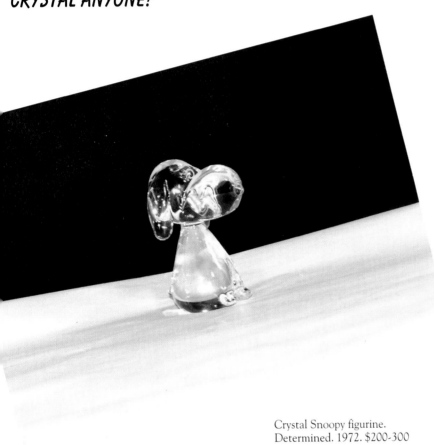

Crystal Snoopy figurine.
Determined. 1972. $200-300

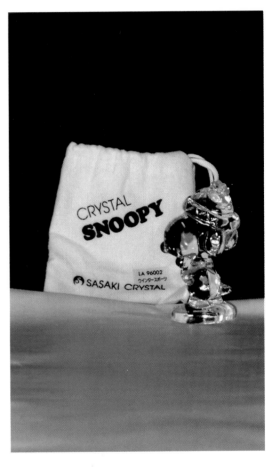

Crystal Snoopy from Sasaki Crystal. Japan. 1990s.
$50-60

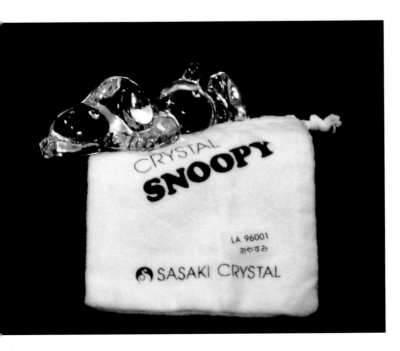

Crystal Snoopy paperweight from Sasaki Crystal.
Japan. 1990s. $50-60

Crystal Snoopy figurine. 21 mm.
Silver Deer. 1990. $50-75

Crystal Snoopy literary Ace. Silver Deer. 1992. $100-125

Silverplate Snoopy bank.
Baseball player. Leonard Silver.
1979. $60-75 w/box

Crystal sitting Snoopy from Sasaki. 1990s. $50-60

Silverplate heart-shaped box by Leonard
Silver Co. 1979. $30-50 w/box

Pewter Snoopy on train from Knott's Berry farms. 1990s. $100-125

Silverplate flower vase with Snoopy hanging on edge. Leonard Silver. 1979. $35-50 w/box

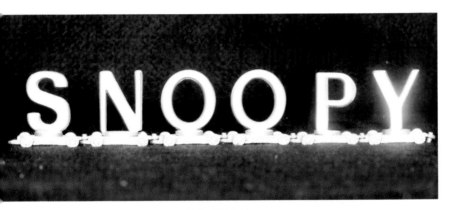

Pewter Snoopy letters forming train. 1990s. $200-225

Limited edition, solid bronze, sculpture set. Original art by Charles Schulz. 1992. Each piece sits on engraved wood base and comes in wooden box. Manufactured by International Trading Technology. Designed by Stan Pawlowski. $750-900 set w/wooden box.

Silverplate baby block bank by Leonard Silver Co. 3" x 3" x 3". 1979. $40-60 w/box

Silver plated Snoopy on dog house bank. Leonard Silver Co. 1979. 6.5". $35-50 w/box

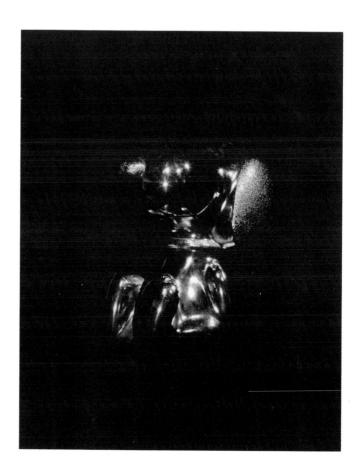

Sitting Snoopy figurine. Leonard. 1979. $35-50

Peanuts silverplated album frame with box. Godinger. Early 1990s. $30-40

Silverplated dresser set by Godinger. 1990. $30-40

Silverplated Snoopy picture frame. Godinger. 1990. $15-25

Silverplated Snoopy doghouse bank by
Godinger. Literary or Flying Ace. 1990.
$20-30 each

Silverplated picture frame. Embossed
dancing Snoopys on rim. Godinger. 1990.
$20-30 w/box

Gold Snoopy necklace. 1980s. $80-110

Brushed gold Snoopy and
Woodstock necklace. Early 1990s.
$150-175

WHAT TIME IS IT?

45th anniversary metal watch from Armitron. Glass dome with ceramic Snoopy on top. 1995. $60-75

Armitron Watch. Mid/late 1990s. This was also a Metlife Premium. $35-50

Flying Ace metal watch with leather band. Armitron. Hands are propellers. 1990. $80-100

Snoopy metal watch with leather band. Armitron. 1990. $80-100

Snoopy plastic watch with plastic band. Armitron. 1990. $30-40

Snoopy metal watch with leather band. Armitron. 1990s. $60-80

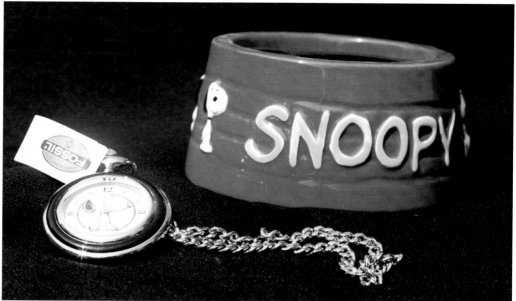

Fossil Special Edition Silver Pocket Watch. Came in ceramic dog dish. $90-100. Also available in gold. $125-150

Peanuts five function digital watch from Armitron. Late 1980s. Non replaceable battery. $5-10

Fossil Special Edition Gold Watch. 1998. Came on resin dog house. $125-150. Also available in silver. $90-110

JEWELRY FOR FUN

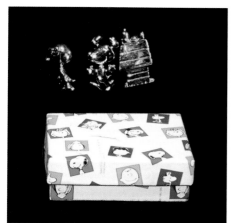

Goldtone and silvertone Snoopy pins. 1". 1990s. $10-15 each

Goldtone Snoopy pin. 2". 1990s. $15-25

Metal enamel Snoopy earring holders. Late 1970s. $15-25 each

Goldtone earrings from Aviva. 1970s. $15-25 each

Snoopy charm on wire necklace. Aviva. 1970s. $15-25

Cloisonne pendant on chain from Aviva. 1970s. $10-20

Peanuts bracelet. Mid-1990s. $40-60

Gold tone character charm bracelet. Enamel. Aviva. 1965. $35-50

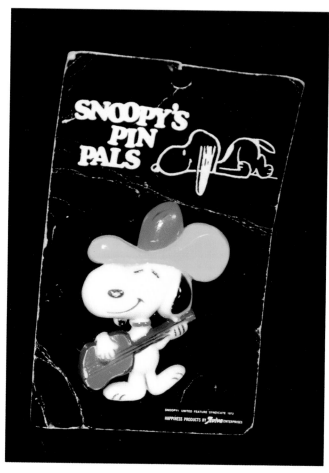

"Snoopy's Pin Pals" from Aviva. 1970s. $20-25

Snoopy NFL Enamel pins, various teams. 1980s. Quantasia. $7-15

Snoopy cloisonne jewelry. 1970s. $20-30 set

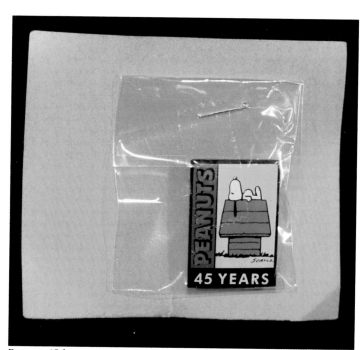

Peanuts 45th year anniversary pin. 1995. $5-10

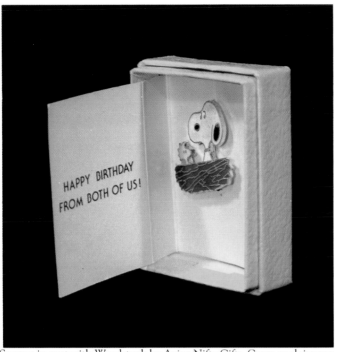

Snoopy in nest with Woodstock by Aviva Nifty Gifts. Came as cloisonne pin or earrings. Early 1970s. $15-25

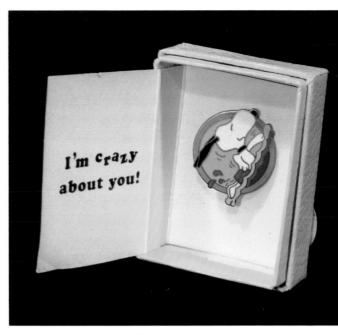

Snoopy surfing by Aviva Nifty Gifts. Came as enamel pin or earrings. Early 1970s. $15-25

Dancing Snoopy by Aviva Nifty Gifts. Came as enamel pin or earrings. Early 1970s. $15-25

Snoopy lapel pins from Aviva. 1970s. $10-20 each on card

Cloisonne Snoopy earrings from Aviva. 1970s. $10-15 pair

Cloisonne Snoopy rings from Aviva. 1970s. $10-15 each

Cloisonne Snoopy pins from Aviva. 1970s. $10-20 each

Cloisonne Snoopy pins from Aviva. 1970s. $10-20 each

*Note: All jewelry originally came on cards.

Plastic, Snoopy for President, flasher button. Move button
and the picture changes to show Snoopy dancing. Hallmark.
Early 1970s. $20-30

Pinbacks by Aviva. Plastic front metal back. Move button
and thepicture changes. 2.5". 1970s. $15-20 each.

Snoopy flasher campaign buttons. "Snoopy for President"
flashes to dancing Snooping. Plastic. Hallmark. Early 1970s.
$20-30. With display $175-200. Button on bottom of house
display. Simon Simple. 1972. Metal 2.5". $20-30. Also
available 1.5" and 0.5" $12-20 each

Pinback with Snoopy and birds from Simon Simple.
1.75". Early 1970s. $15-30

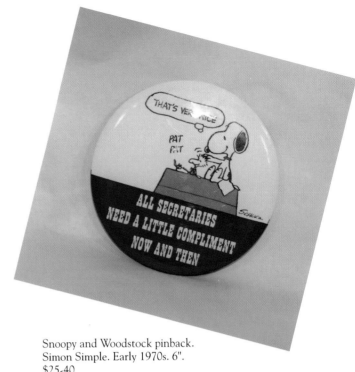

Snoopy and Woodstock pinback.
Simon Simple. Early 1970s. 6".
$25-40

12 pinbacks. Metal 1.5" each sold
seperately. Early 1970s. Simon Simple.
$20-30 each

Metal pinback. 1.75". Early 1970s.
Simon Simple. $15-30

"Snoopy for President" pin. 1970s.
$15-25

"Knott's Camp Snoopy"
pin. 1990s. $5-7

"Snoopy Fan Club" pin.
1980s. $5-10

Snoopy pin. "Love Me."
Butterfly. 1980s. $5-10

Plastic "Blarney Beagle"
pin. 1980s. $5-10

SPECIAL STUFF

Cotton "Apollo 11 Lunar Team" patch. 25th Anniversary. $75-100

Camp Snoopy collectors coins from Knott's Berry Farm. Grand Opening of Camp Snoopy in Bloomington, Minnesota. Nickel silver. 1992. $6-10

Plastic phone cards. Steve Young from San Francisco 49ers. Made by ATT. "Snoopy Bowl." 1995. $15-20 each

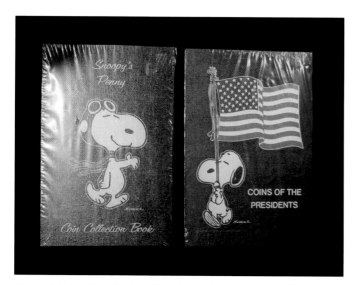

Coins of the Presidents book. 1970s. Snoopy's penny coin collection book. Jerry Briskin Enterprises. $25-35 each

1998 McDonalds fast food chain is having riots over this silly toy. They want 28 articulating fun figures. They are 3"-3 1/4" tall and depict Snoopy dressed in traditional clothing for different cultures. Don't worry if you do not know all the cultures as they are marked on the bottom of his foot. Complete sets of this collection sold for a short time for thousands of dollars on the black market. Thank goodness the frenzy subsided so the average collector might afford this set. $200-350 mint set with case.

ADVERTISING WITH OUR FAVORITE BEAGLE!

Metlife began advertising with Snoopy as early as 1987.

Advertising poster from Metlife. Early 1990s. (Sent out free when requested). $4-7

Metlife advertising pin. 1980s/90s. $10-15

Cardboard Metlife advertising. 5 feet tall. Mid-1990s. $50-75

Advertising playing cards from Metlife. 1990s. $10-12

Advertising kite from Metlife.
This was a free promotional kite.
1990s. $2-3

Plastic frisbies from Metlife. 1990s. $5-7 each

Advertising balloon from Metlife. 1990s.
$1-2

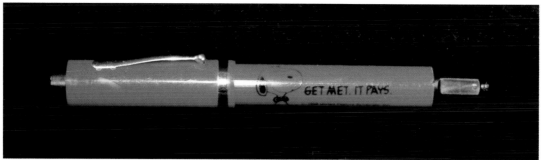

Advertising pen from Metlife. 1990s. $5-10

Ceramic advertising cups from Metlife. 1990s. $10-15 each

Advertising plastic ice scraper
from Metlife. 1980s/1990s. $7-10

Plastic covered mug from
Metlife. 1980s/1990s. $6-8

Nylon Brock-a-brella from Metlife. 1980s. $12-15

Fabric carry-all from Metlife. St. Louis Cardinals logo. $10-20 mint

Fabric carry-all from Metlife. Throughout the late 1980s/1990s Metlife sponsored many sports events with wonderful totebags. $10-20 mint

Plastic and metal advertising key chain from Metlife. 1990s. $6-10 each

Advertising key chains from Metlife. 1980s/1990s. $6-8 each

Luggage tag from Metlife. 1990s. $4-6

"A Family's Guide to Child Safety" Metlife. (Was sent out free when requested). 1990s. $1-2

"Chex Party Mix" advertising label. 1990s. $1-2

A&W began advertising with Snoopy as early as 1989 and continued only through 1994.

Cardboard advertising banner from A & W rootbeer. 6' long 12" deep. 1990s. $3-5

Aluminum 6 pack cans of Snoopy soda from A & W root beer. Early to mid-1990s. Came in Cream soda and in regular or diet. 6 pack-full. $10-20

Plastic cups from A & W rootbeer. 1990s. $15-20 set

173

Snoopy video tank topper advertising for Shell Oil. 1993. $7-10

Cardboard banner from card display. Hallmark. 1970s. $10-15

Snoopy in Uncle Sam top hat. Interstate Brands (Dolly Madison, Weber's Bread, Butternut, Mrs. Karl's). Four shrink wrapped posters include other characters. Promotional. 1970s. $25-40 set

Snoopy for President pin. $10-15

Snoopy's gallery and gift shop pin. 1980s. $4-6

Advertising round sticker for
Snoopy Shoes. 1970s. $3-4

Snoopy for President pin. 1970s. $10-15

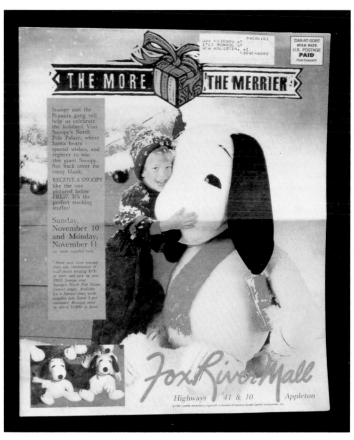

Advertising from Fox River Mall. Mid-1990s. $1-2

Suncoast Christmas ad. 1994. $1-2

Advertising from National Golf
Federation. Golf course etiquette.
1995. $1-2

noopy decals from Dolly Madison. 1980s. $5-7